READERS LO...

Feathers B...

My Heart

"If only I could tell you how much your book changed my life and the lives in my motherless daughters group. The hope and inspiration it has brought is difficult to put into words."
—Heather McConnell (Carol's daughter),
Nicoma Park, OK

"I purchased FEATHERS just three weeks after my mother suddenly died. It has helped to maintain my sanity while I try to gain my balance."
—Sherry Bell, Ph.D., Sedona, AR

"As I go through the second year without my mama I have been at such a standstill with my grief drowning me most days! And now with Mother's Day heckling me everywhere I turn it's been hard to find a place to come up for air. With the discovery of your book I found a place! Thank you and God bless you."
—Melissa Little, Phoenix, AZ

"When I finished FEATHERS BRUSH MY HEART, I actually hugged the book and kissed it. I then knew for certain my mother is with me.... Your book put all of this together for me. I thought maybe I was making it up because of my terrible need for my mother. I feel validated. Thanks so much.... I know this book didn't come into my path by accident."
—Judith Ann Burton, Merced, CA

more...

"The most significant message that came through did so in your book. One night after sitting at the computer and crying, I asked my mother to come to me....I pulled myself together to begin reading your book again. I think I was on page 132, my mother's house number, when I turned the page and read the lines 'Kim, my youngest daughter.' I knew my mother was trying to comfort me....Thank you so much for writing this book."
—Kim Monocchi, Hamden, CT

"One Sunday morning while home alone, I opened this book and remembered the yellow finch (from four years earlier after asking for a sign)....I put the book down, walked to the French doors, and said aloud, 'Mama, was that you?' Instantly two bright yellow finches landed on my patio in the pouring rain, looked directly at me, then flew away. I burst into tears, crying, 'Thank you, Mom, you finally touched me.' I think she even brought my father along."
—Jessie Bercot, Lafayette, OH

"Thank you so much for the book....You will not be surprised, I'm sure, to learn that I had a dream about my late wife, Terri, only a day or two after the book arrived. What a lovely gift."
—David Corbett, Vallejo, CA

Feathers Brush My Heart

TRUE STORIES OF MOTHERS
TOUCHING THEIR DAUGHTERS' LIVES
AFTER DEATH

Sinclair Browning

WARNER BOOKS

An AOL Time Warner Company

The publishers have generously given permission to use extended quotations from the following copyrighted works. From *Practical Intuition*, © 1996 by Laura Day. Reprinted by permission of Random House. From *The Eagle and the Rose*, © 1996 by Rosemary Altea. Reprinted by permission of Warner Books. From *The Road Less Traveled and Beyond*, © 1997 by M. Scott Peck, M.D. Reprinted by permission of Simon and Schuster.
See page 277 for complete contributions copyright information.

Warner Books, Inc., 1271 Avenue of the Americas, New York, NY 10020

Visit our Web site at www.twbookmark.com.

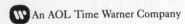 An AOL Time Warner Company

Printed in the United States of America
Originally published in hardcover by Warner Books, Inc.
First Trade Printing: April 2003
10 9 8 7 6 5 4 3 2 1

The Library of Congress has cataloged the hardcover edition as follows:

Feathers brush my heart : true stories of mothers touching their daughters' lives after death / [compiled by] Sinclair Browning.
    p. cm.
  Includes bibliographical references.
  ISBN 0-446-52819-6
    1. Spiritualism. 2. Mothers and daughters. I. Browning, Sinclair.

BF1275.W65 F43 2002
133.9'082—dc21   2001046534

ISBN: 0-446-69081-3 (pbk.)

Book design by Giorgetta Bell McRee
Cover design by Jackie Merri Meyer
Photograph by Robert Holmgren/Tony Stone Images

For my mother . . .
and yours

Sometimes I think, what would I do if my mother dies? She is the longest and most important relationship in my life. More than any man I've ever had. More than my own children and my grandchildren. Because she was with me before I was born and she has been with me always with unconditional love. All the other loves that I have had are conditional.

—ISABEL ALLENDE
Wings of Love

Contents ∼

Genesis ～

I am fifty-five years old. I have had broken bones, had stitches, given birth, lost my father when I was eleven, had a home burn to the ground, been divorced, lost close friends, and buried all of my grandparents as well as my ex-husband.

But none of it compares to the grief I felt when my mother died. That was a pain that was so deep, so wrenching, that the scar tissue still wraps my heart. It no longer threatens to strangle me, for the wound is now softened from time to time with my mother's afterlife gifts to me.

It is only recently that I have come to understand that my mother's gifts are not unique, that mothers everywhere send their children gifts from the afterlife. Unfortunately, we don't always receive them. Sometimes our radios are turned too low; more frequently we question what we instinctively know. In her book *The Secret Language of Signs*, Denise Linn says that in every moment the universe is whispering to us. There are signs everywhere, personal messages from a world beyond our own.

But let me go back to the birth of this book.

Every year I go on an all-women's horseback ride. This is a great concept—125 women and their horses camped out in the pines of northern Arizona. It is always a fun-filled four days, with campfires, catered meals, and lots of talk and laughter. Sort of like a giant slumber party for grown-ups.

One trip a few years ago was no different and yet it was very, very different.

Late at night, with the moon turning bloodred in eclipse, my friend Linda Gray and I begin talking. As the night wears on, she tells me a wonderful story about her mother's afterlife gifts.

After her mother's death a butterfly perched on Linda's shoulder.

"I knew it was from my mother," she says.

That started a steady stream of shoulder perchers, later followed by hummingbirds. I will not relate the story here, for Linda does it better justice in "Soul Birds."

When she finishes her story, I tell Linda about my experience with my mother's afterlife gifts.

"You know," Linda says, "I'm usually the one telling the story, and here you are telling me one."

Suddenly it hits me. If we have these stories, surely there must be other women who have had similar experiences. I go to bed, excited at the prospect.

I awaken in the middle of the night and begin taking notes. Suddenly a book begins to take form.

Over coffee the next morning a friend who is camped next to me says, "You know, I could hear some of your conversation last night and it sounded so interesting. I really wanted to get out of bed and join in, but it was too cold. What were you talking about?"

Another friend joins us, and I as speak to them of butterflies and hummingbirds, they both begin to cry.

That night, during the cocktail hour, I mention the subject to two elderly sisters who come on this annual trek. One of them begins telling her story. They are both crying. By now I know that my chance conversation with Linda has evolved into something so powerful, so strong, that it strikes a deep, resonant chord in all of our hearts.

I go to Carroll Gabrielson's motor home, where she sits with another woman. Carroll is in charge of the ride.

"I want to talk to you about something, and if I'm out of line, I want you to tell me."

Carroll assures me that she will.

I tell a little about my mother and her gift to me, and say I am thinking of writing a book. And then I take a deep breath.

"I'm wondering if I could get up tonight and tell a little about the project and see if any of the women here have similar stories."

I'm apprehensive. Rejection is never pleasant.

It is only when Carroll reaches into an overhead bin and pulls down a box of Kleenex that I realize that she and the other woman are crying.

She, of course, thinks it is a wonderful idea.

After the program that night, under the northern Arizona stars with campfires flickering and women huddled around them, I begin to speak. I tell about my mother's afterlife gift as though it were the most natural topic in the world. It's dark and I cannot see many of the women. I'm somewhat afraid that I am throwing a damper on the evening. After all, who likes to talk about death? As I walk back to my seat several women stop me.

"We have stories," they say. And the sharing begins.

A woman approaches me.

"I'm going to tell you a story," she begins. "I have told it to very few people because most won't understand or they will scoff at it. After hearing you, I want to share it because I know you will know what it means."

She has said it all. These are secret stories. Stories we whisper to one another under the cover of night. Stories we pass on with the caveat, "You'll never believe this, but . . ."

Years ago my husband had a friend, Charlie, who was quite ill. On his deathbed Charlie vowed that if there was a way to tell my husband that things were all right where he was going, he would do so. Months passed and whenever I asked my husband about Charlie, he'd laugh and say, "He hasn't called yet."

Then one morning he awakened and said, "You know, I had the strangest dream about Charlie last night. I was walking through a park and he was sitting on a bench reading the newspaper. I sat down next to him and said, 'Charles, how's it going?' and he replied, 'Everything's just fine here.'"

My husband doubted that this was a message. I didn't. I've since learned that one of the easiest ways for spirits to communicate with us is through our dreams. It is also one of the easiest ways for us to understand their messages.

The poet Samuel Taylor Coleridge wrote an interesting passage on dreams. He said:

What if you slept? And what if, in your sleep, you dreamed? And what if, in your dream, you went to heaven and there plucked a beautiful flower? And what if, when you awoke, you had the flower in your hand? Ah, what then?

There is no question that seeing our mothers, whether in vision or dream form, is a powerful thing. After my mother died, at times, for no apparent reason, I'd tear through the house desperately seeking a picture of her. It was almost as though I needed to remember what she looked like. Then, when she came to me in dreams, that was even better, for she was even more real. She walked and talked and had all of the endearing mannerisms that I remembered about her.

Since ancient times, people have studied their dreams in an effort to delve into personal exploration. Dreams are also one of the easiest ways for spirits to communicate with those of us still in the physical world.

Some mothers have appeared as visions, others in dreams. It's not uncommon for the mother to appear in a much younger incarnation than the age she was when she died. In some cases, she has appeared not only at a younger age, but one that the daughter did not recognize! The common denominator here seems to be health. Regardless of what the mother died of, no matter how devastating the death, she appears healthy, happy, and whole, with a spiritual glow about her. Mothers trapped in wheelchairs walk and those shriveled from cancer are vibrant again. This is a great gift for those of us who have lost our loved ones to debilitating disease.

I believe that as women, we are the intuitive ones. We must constantly be open to things we do not understand. To receive, without question. To trust our hearts. In *The Little Prince*, Antoine de Saint-Exupéry writes, "It is with the heart that one sees rightly; what is essential is invisible to the eye."

On an earthier note, it's kind of like seeing a mountain lion. Years ago I was feeding my horses early one morning and I caught a flash of color. Later I told my brother Lance, "You know, I saw this thing, but I didn't really see it, but I think maybe it was a mountain lion."

"If you thought it was, it probably was," he said.

If you think you're getting a message or a gift, you probably are.

I don't know what the ethics are in all of this spirit business. Maybe there are rules that say you can't pick up the chalk and leave the message on the board. But I do know that the more we talk, the better off we are all going to be. If we, as women, share these feathers that brush our hearts, we will start a spiritual revolution that will rival any that has come before.

Seventy women, from varied geographical locations, occupations, and ethnicities, have contributed stories to this book. Not all of the women have had great relationships with their mothers before they died. One woman was so abused that she still bears scars from her mother "teaching" her to stay out of the kitchen.

Like their contributors, the afterlife gifts are diverse, ranging from tangible objects to visions and dreams, from sounds and smells to life-saving warnings.

For the last three years, I've shared the wonderful stories that have come my way with those who believe, while opening the realm of possibility to those who do not. Women have found catharsis and healing not only in writing the stories, but also in hearing them. By sharing the afterlife gift stories, many of which go far beyond mere chance, we get a definition of what lies beyond death. Contributor Sandra Heater, Ph.D., writes:

> I was having a lot of trouble with losing my mother and completing the grieving process. It was a very difficult emotional thing for me to do. Unfortunately, there's no way to rehearse that loss. You feel totally bereft and nothing else quite fills that void. Reading other women's stories about their connections with their mothers is a validation for me. When something that is extraordinary and forceful and inexplicable happens on one level, I am reassured that these things do occur. Any time we go into an unknown realm, there's a human need to be

reassured that it's all right to be where we are. These are affirmations that what happened to me . . . was not a figment of my imagination.

Feathers Brush My Heart has gone from an idea one dark night to the book that is now in your hands. I must say it's been a whirlwind odyssey.

One of my discoveries during the process has been that the subject of death is not a gruesome one. For what we call death is only a door opening to a place we will never really understand until it is our time to be there. Those who have crossed that threshold do not cease to exist. They are as real in their world as we are in ours. And, if we're lucky, and aware, what comes through after death from those loved ones who have gone before are gifts of love, humor, and hope.

This journey has also taught me another important lesson: It only takes one.

One person to come forward, without embarrassment or fear of censure, and say, "This is what happened to me, and I am not afraid to tell you about it."

By sharing, we open our hearts to one another, and there is no greater power on the face of this earth.

In closing, I would like to encourage each of you to share your stories. Each telling will get easier, I promise. And as you share, perhaps more and more people will come out into this open field, and all of our stories, singly and collectively, will raise the consciousness of our great, glorious world.

Peace and faith be with you.

SINCLAIR BROWNING

Finding Your Truth ~

We create the software for our soul.

—DEEPAK CHOPRA

The stories you are about to read are as individual as the people who are telling them. While not all of the contributors are writers, each has a story to tell, written from her heart.

Whatever the standards are in the spirit world, there is no doubt that there are many ways to receive an afterlife gift. Recipients have found actual physical objects or animals, felt a touch, heard voices or other aural messages, smelled something, or had visions of the loved one. These gifts may come when the receiver is asleep, dreaming, or partially or fully awake.

Much of what comes in may seem inconsequential. That's true even in the stories that appear here. However, the messages you may receive, even the most seemingly insignificant ones, are remarkable when you consider that they are gifts from dead people. That's right. Someone you are close to has died and has thoughtfully sent you a gift from the world beyond. Now, that alone is pretty incredible!

So what kind of an afterlife gift are you likely to receive? And how important will it be in the great scheme of things?

Receiving tangible gifts is fairly common. While there

is nothing particularly significant about a white feather, a red hair ribbon, or an antique vase, when the recipient recognizes that its appearance was not by mere chance but was a message from her mother, then all of these objects become reverent. There is nothing inconsequential about gifts that so profoundly affect their recipients.

I remember cleaning out my mother's house after she died. We couldn't find the title to her car. We all knew she kept it in her glove compartment, but our thorough searches of her Taurus were futile. We then attacked every closet, drawer, jacket pocket, filing cabinet, and empty purse and still had no luck. After a day or two of madly hunting for it, we finally gave up and sat on the porch drinking lemonade, lamenting the fact that the car title was apparently irretrievably lost.

Five minutes later my sister went outside and found the title sitting on the hood of Mother's car. Of course, each of us immediately accused the other three of playing a trick. And, not surprisingly since none of us had anything at all to do with it, we all denied the accusation.

Unusual? I thought so until these stories came in. Now I've learned that our mothers can be very helpful when it comes to dredging up lost objects.

There are a number of other ways that spirits communicate with us. We may smell a perfume, roses, or even medicine that was associated with our mothers. We're buying a new house (or publishing a book!) and everything goes smoothly, as though it's meant to be.

Frequently a mother will come to say good-bye either shortly before or after she dies, or even at the moment of death. These good-byes may occur whether a person has a lingering death or one that is sudden and unexpected. Distances are unimportant in the spirit world, and often the news of a leave-taking travels great miles. While the news might be received at a certain time in one time zone, when it is translated into the time of the locale where the person died, it is usually the exact time of death.

While we've come to trust our five senses, it's important to remember that soul communication does not always come through in this way. You may not find a lost object or receive a physical sign or an auditory message. Sometimes the communication transcends all of these things, and there is just a *knowing* on the part of the recipient. Your mother is communicating her love and warmth and wisdom to you and you are engulfed in it. There's no logical explanation for what you are sensing, but you *know* that what you are feeling is a gift from your mother.

Vibrations in the spirit world are much faster than the vibrations here at the physical level on earth. This is the reason that many mediums, such as James Van Praagh, sometimes have trouble exactly interpreting what comes through. On the one hand, you have the spirit who is trying to slow down so her message can be heard; on the other, you have the living person who is trying to still her mind so the new frequency can come in.

It's important to trust the thoughts and feelings that you get. When you experience a feeling that tells you that your mother is around, honor it. Learn to trust your own intuition and feelings.

When it comes to afterlife gifts, one thing is clear: There are no clear rules. There is no right or wrong way to either send a communication or receive one. While this particular book focuses on afterlife gifts mothers have sent their daughters, these stories could be from any spirit to anyone on earth.

JUNE FIRST

Sinclair Browning

Sinclair Browning, fifty-five, lives in Tucson, Arizona. A professional writer, she is the author of the Trade Ellis mystery series and several historical novels and is the coauthor of a horse-training book, *Lyons on Horses*.

All of us, of course, knew that she was failing. She was weaker each day as the pain grew stronger. The morphine increased, and her periods of lucidity shrank. Clearly, it was only a matter of time.

We had celebrated her sixty-fifth birthday just two days before, and flowers and balloons still decked the room. One balloon, the latest in such latex innovations, sported bouncing arms and legs, a lecherous smile, *Happy Birthday* tattooed across its forehead, and penny loafers.

We soon discovered that if we placed nickels in his shoes, this would provide a necessary anchor, and we could walk him around. And walk him we did. Past patients' rooms, up to the nurses' station during early morning hours, and sometimes we would just tape him to the walls of Room 1063 to give him a break. The Happy Man, we called him, as he brought cheer into otherwise bleak hours.

And, lest anyone tells you otherwise, the deathwatch, while instructional, is not fun.

As the morphine wore off, Mother would cry and whimper in pain. It drove us crazy. The clock ruled her suffering. Is it time for another injection? No, not quite. Here, have something else. Not as good as morphine. Maddening. Sometimes, through the pain and the hallucinations, a clear thought would emerge.

I thought I was hearing one two nights earlier when Mother sat straight up in her bed. "Oh, thank you, thank you, thank you," she gushed.

"For what?" I asked, pleased that I had unwittingly done something nice for her.

"The gift. The precious, precious gift you have given me. The wonderful gift you have given the world. Thank you, thank you, thank you."

My mind raced. The gift? My son? My books? I didn't like the puzzle, so I had to ask, "What gift, Mother?"

"Why, thank you for killing me," she said with a beatific smile on her face.

What had the drugs done to my beautiful mother? I'd given her nothing. I wasn't killing her, the cancer was.

The medicine finally arrived.

A nurse came in and suggested a morphine drip. Oh, it's so much better, she assured us. Puts a steady dose right in. Keeps them comfortable and they can still be aware.

In retrospect, that's the one question I have. Once the morphine machine arrived and was hooked up, Mother never spoke again. Did we do the right thing? I don't know. Is relief from pain in exchange for communication a fair trade? Would the words have evaporated anyway? They say so. But I don't know. It's something we should have discussed with Mother. And didn't.

And while the family had always been close, I never thought of us as hovering. But hover we did. Each child staking out his or her place, standing sentinel over the shell that was once our mother.

She'd kicked nearly everyone out of her room at one time or another. Claustrophobia, she said. And we had no reason to doubt her, for we'd all suffered occasionally from the same affliction. But now she could not shoo us away, for she could not speak. And, like circling jackals, we moved in, each one of us convinced that lacking the magic to save her, we alone were the path to her salvation.

For two days now I had watched my brothers—is it a male thing?—stroke, stroke, stroke Mother's forehead. What had started out as a touching gesture had now evolved into an addiction. As Lance's blond male hand left, George's brunette one charged. Stroke, stroke, stroke. I prayed her forehead was not sore, although I knew it must be. My heart wrestled with my brain as I considered my role. Mother protector? Brother comforter? Hurt one, save the other. What choice? Silently I watched the hulks hover and stroke.

Mother, of course, said nothing.

Several friends shared with me that their parents, who also succumbed to cancer, quit drinking water three days before they died. Eagerly I looked for this sign that would only come the last day. The day before she died, Mother was still able to suck up two full straws of water. After her final sip we resorted to placing our fingers over the top of the straw, creating a vacuum that would pull the water up, and then we would carefully deposit our lode into her dry mouth. We'd known this system since childhood and the paradox hit us as we employed it now. Instead of making a scrunched-up straw wrapper walk, we now treated each drop as the magic elixir that would bring Mother back to life. Of course, it didn't work.

Finally the straw was no longer safe. She could no longer swallow. The next order of business, according to the nurses who knew such things, was a sponge swab, dampened with water and rubbed around the tongue and the inside of the mouth. A lousy substitute for a drink of water, we all agreed.

As dawn broke on the first of June the real downhill

slide began. Blood pressure 50 over 30. It doesn't go much lower than that, the nurse volunteered. Pulse? Where is it?

No one left for breakfast.

Happy Man now stood on the adjacent hospital bed, his smiling face beaming down at Mother.

"We should put that at the foot of her bed," I suggested.

"God, no, that would scare her to death," one of my brothers argued.

"Well?" I said. It was our last laugh for hours.

The decline continued throughout the morning. Each new measurement brought lower pressures as her strong heart vibrated her tiny chest, working overtime to keep the program that it had run for so long, alive.

I wondered why she was staying. "Let's leave Mother alone for a few minutes," I suggested.

My siblings moved in closer. "No way," they chorused.

"She's been in this place for three weeks and has not been alone a single moment," I argued my point. "Maybe this is something she wants to do alone."

We'd been into charades all morning. Mother, if you want some water, blink. Mother, if you're in pain, blink. Mother, should we leave you alone, blink. Blink. Don't blink. Blink.

I had watched the signals pretty intensely, and a strong case could be made for either side. The blinks were ambiguous at best.

A few more minutes passed before I repeated my suggestion. Finally, with support from my sister, my brothers conceded and we all retreated to the hall, leaving Mother a to-the-minute-by-the-watch two minutes alone.

It didn't work.

We filed back in. A drawer yielded a Bible and my sister began reciting particularly apt passages. I stumbled through several hymns. One by one we all thanked

Mother for the many things she had given us throughout our lives—love, integrity, support, art, knowledge, manners. All were recited as we watched the life ebb from the woman who alone had raised us.

She twitched and we worried that she was in pain. A nurse was called in.

After a quick examination, she proclaimed that the end was near. The blood is pooling in her torso, there is no blood pressure or pulse, there is no pain. No, I can't give her anything.

I panicked. I wanted to shield this woman, who had given me so much, from everything. If it was in my power to thwart her pain, then I would do it. Lacking God's intervention, I needed the power of the hospital icon. I called the doctor.

He valiantly came to my mental rescue as he assured me that what I was seeing was the body continuing to do what it had been programmed to do. Mother was removed from her pain, removed from her body. My tears stopped as he talked me through her dying. I could not thank him enough.

As her breathing became more shallow, we began saying our good-byes. A tear escaped from her eye, and we knew that it was her farewell to us. There was no death rattle that noon.

"Good-bye, Mother," I said as she drew her last breath. While the day had been still, a breeze rustled at the window.

"Yeah, Mother!" Giving it my high school best, I turned to the ceiling, knowing she was watching all of us from somewhere Up There. "Have a good trip! Go with God."

"We love you," my sister sobbed.

"Go to the light," one of my brothers encouraged.

The first time I went to a funeral and heard it called a celebration, I thought it charming. Now, having attended too many such celebrations, I find the term not only trite, but irritating. That day, though, we were truly celebrating. It was a sad celebration, but a celebration nonetheless.

The nurse came in and told us what we already knew. We asked for a few minutes alone as we each said a prayer and yet another good-bye.

Then came the routine stuff. Clear out the hospital room. Why hadn't we thought to diminish the possessions before now? It would have been so easy to take a few things home at a time instead of this marshaling of resources and bags to vacate a three-week stay. Plans were arranged for meeting at our grandmother's house. Mortuaries consulted. Flowers given away.

The balloons we saved until the last. Taking them outside, we encircled them as we celebrated yet another time. Happy Man, by mutual consent, was to go home to be introduced to two of the small grandchildren. He had given us so much happiness in an otherwise unhappy time, we could not bear to part with him quite so freely. We would, in time, find out why.

As we released other balloons from her room into the clear, hot Arizona sky, we each felt a release within ourselves. Mother was soaring with the balloons, with the eagles, with God now. Her soul was released, as they were, and she was now free to fly.

The evening of June 1, everyone came for dinner. The children had a wonderful time with Happy Man, now somewhat the worse for wear with an amputated arm reattached with Scotch tape.

"Let's let him go," someone suggested.

We all agreed that it was the proper thing to do. In preparation for his flight, we removed the nickels from Happy Man's loafers. As we released him, only a slight breeze teased the clear twilight.

The balloon wafted upward and then floated to the

north for a few feet. Casually he settled into the high limbs of a chinaberry tree, his back to his appreciative audience.

"Oh, he's not facing us," my grandmother said.

As if on cue, Happy Man drifted up above the tree again, and while there was no earthly reason why he should not have continued his upward passage, he chose instead to return again to the tree, only this time he settled in facing the family.

Although the breeze did not warrant such action, he waved his arms gaily before sailing up into the warm Arizona night.

Tears streamed down my face as I said what I thought would be my last good-bye.

I was numb those first few days. And then the real pain set in. Pain so searing, so devastating that I thought my heart would break. Just when I thought I had things under control, another arrow would come from out of nowhere and pierce me yet again. I'd be in the market and see the back of a woman's head that, for a fleeting moment, I thought was my mother. And then I'd remember. Once, while driving home, I spotted a white Taurus in front of me. Mother's dropping by, I thought. And then I'd remember. And with each occurrence, the pain I thought was ebbing would swell and roll over me once again, threatening to bury me in the deepest grief I'd ever known.

Several weeks after Mother's death I went out to feed the horses one morning and found the swimming pool covered with white feathers. Intuitively I knew they were from Mother. While my ranch had chickens, there had been no coyote raids and the fowl were healthy. Thereafter white feathers would appear from time to time.

But why feathers?

Finally I remembered. My mother had been an aspiring actress before she married my father. As part of her theatrical training she would lie on the floor and blow a white feather up in the air and say "I love you" before the feather came down. On its descent she would exhale and send it airborne once again while repeating "I love you." The whole purpose of the exercise was to build her diaphragm so she could project as an actress. After that, while I never thought that every white feather I saw was sent by my mother, instinctively I knew exactly which ones were. They were her way of telling me that she loved me and that she was fine.

My husband laughed at the notion until he found a white feather on his workbench, in his car, on his coat, in his desk drawer.

Six weeks after my mother's death I went to lunch with two close friends who had known my mother well. They asked me how I was doing. "Fine," I replied. "She's sending me white feathers."

They blanched.

"This morning," my friend Colistia began, "I had the kitchen doors open so a breeze could come through the house. A cactus wren flew in the open doors. After I shooed him out with a broom, I found a white feather on the floor."

Cactus wrens are not known for their white plumage.

My other dear friend Lynn nodded and began talking.

"When I was making the bed this morning, I found a white feather in the middle of it."

Lynn does not use down pillows or feather linens.

The feathers have kept coming over the years. Not long ago my brother Lance went through a devastating divorce. As he was leaving my house after a particularly disturbing day, he spotted a perfect white feather on a bush. He knew it was from Mother, telling him she was with him. During the writing of this book, Mother has sent feathers not only to me, but also to many of the participants.

On a recent visit my sister, Rowena, and I went horseback riding. As we crossed the dry creek behind the house, there was a large white fluffy feather on the ground. At once we both said, "Mother!" Rowena picked up the feather and put it in her hat. As she did so, I thought, *There's no way that feather is going to stay there for two hours.* Miraculously, it did. When we returned and were putting up the horses, my sister was leading her horse into the pasture and the feather drifted high up into the air, above her head, and began falling down on the far side of the horse. As she opened the gate, the feather drifted down and landed on her shoe! Just another way of Mother's letting us know that she was with us. Thinking back on this now, I'm laughing. Mother was afraid of horses, and that was probably the closest she ever got to one!

Each time I see these special white feathers, they speak to me. They are not always on special anniversaries, and I cannot say that there is a rhyme or reason to them. There doesn't have to be.

It is enough that they are there.

They have taught me that "good-bye" is a transient word. For once souls have touched, they can never disconnect. There will always be signs—whether a vase in a painting, a mysterious woman in a doorway, or a hummingbird with its bill stuck in a screen just long enough—these are all feathers that brush our hearts.

BUTTERFLY LOVE

Glennis Sanger Firestone

Glennis Sanger Firestone is currently working on her family genealogy. Her other hobbies include reading and music. Glennis, forty-six, shares her life with her husband, two children, and a granddaughter.

My mother and I had a pretty typical mother/daughter relationship. She was the kind of mom who based her life on her children. She didn't work outside the home, other than a couple of times, and then it wasn't for long.

Perhaps it was because my mother lost a baby between my sister and me that she lived for her children. We were kids who grew up never having a baby-sitter. Not once.

While my mother was my best friend, there was also a kind of sisterhood between us. I think it's a sisterhood that all women share, or should share, because we are women.

When my mother got sick, she stayed with us in the house that we are now living in, and we took care of her. During the last six months of her life we went through the hospice program with her. I found myself among very spiritual people, and my mother was one of them. This was a very emotional, very intense time for all of us.

My mother's illness was serious and terminal. It was very stressful for me because no matter what I tried to do, I couldn't make her better. I didn't understand that for a long time.

About three weeks to a month before my mother died, I was lying in bed one night watching TV when a misty cloud rolled into the room and floated in front of the television. It wanted to make sure that it was seen and heard.

While it wasn't detailed, didn't look like a person or have a body or facial features, I somehow knew that it was a beautiful angel. When I first saw it, I was scared because I didn't know what was happening, but then I heard it and felt it and it spoke to me.

The angel told me that it would be over soon and that I should take care of my mother. It told me to help my sister deal with our mother's death and then assured me that everything would be OK.

I felt better after that.

Before my mother died, she told my father that she would come back as a butterfly. My mother was part Cherokee and I know that in that particular tribe, as well as in some others, butterflies signify rebirth.

It was only after her death that my father shared the butterfly story with me. When we scattered my mother's ashes two days later at the cemetery, I brought some of them home to place beneath my rosebushes.

As soon as I got done scattering them, there came a butterfly. A single black butterfly. Until my mother's death we've never had a lot of butterflies out here. I don't doubt for a minute that the butterfly was my mother telling me that everything was all right.

And now, every time we go to the cemetery there's always a butterfly. Always black. Always just one.

My granddaughter Marissa knows the butterfly story. We were driving by the cemetery where my mother's ashes are buried not long ago when she said, "Let's go see Me Me."

In the cemetery rose garden there are plaques with names on them. When I asked if she knew which one was her grandmother's, she pointed right to it although she had never seen the place before and is too young to read. We sat on a bench waiting for the black butterfly, and of course, on that day as on all others, one appeared.

Marissa talks a lot about my mother. She'll suddenly look up at the sky and say, "There's Me Me. There's Me Me! Can't you see her?"

MADLEE

Madelyn Smith

Madelyn Smith, fifty-six, is the cofounder of two family businesses. Married for thirty-six years, Madelyn acknowledges that her greatest gifts are her family and friends.

My mother suffered from Alzheimer's for nine years prior to her death in 1996. This disease robbed her of her ability to communicate or recognize her family. My sister and I remained close to her in her last years, although it was a difficult and stressful experience.

Mother and I had a good relationship. She was dynamite, constantly on the go, a real Auntie Mame. While Mother was loving, she was not touchy or cuddly. The tender moments we shared were very private and reserved for the most serious illness or grave circumstance.

About eight months after my mother's death, my husband was out of town for several nights. My habit when he was gone was to stay up until around 1 A.M., when I would fall into bed, exhausted.

I have sleep apnea, a condition that causes me to awaken frequently each night with my heart racing, gasping for breath, experiencing a feeling of terror. For this condition I sleep using a machine that forces air into my nose and throat, providing even and constant breathing. My apnea causes me to fall asleep suddenly and deeply, often while driving or during conversations.

I was sleeping on my back when my deceased mother called to me and touched me. She appeared to be around age thirty-four, as she might have been during my youth, but I do not remember ever seeing her with dark brown hair and such a youthful face. In her last years she was an emaciated, small, uncommunicative woman in her seventies.

The warmth from her touch, which did not hurt, lasted several minutes and extended deep into my shoulder. It was unlike anything I had ever felt before. While I was not afraid, I did take this as a warning. And then she spoke.

While her presence and warmth probably would have been enough to awaken me immediately, the name she called—"Madlee"—brought me wide awake. I honestly do not even know how the name should be spelled, since I doubt my mother called me by this name more than a few times in my life. If I had been asked if I had a nickname, I would not have remembered it. Yet on this evening I was Madlee, a name my mother used only during the most tender, unguarded moments. The one time I can remember her calling me by the name was when I had spinal meningitis at sixteen and was the only one in the state with the disease.

I awakened suddenly and totally. I lay in my bed feeling the warmth and willing her to contact me again. She did not.

As I lay there for several minutes thinking, I tried to interpret the meaning of my mother's appearance. She was trying to warn me about something, but what? I got up and walked through the house checking all the doors and windows and found them secure. I eventually returned to bed, put on the C-Pap breathing machine, and was soon asleep.

The next day I shared my experience with my son, Todd. He asked if I had been using my breathing machine. I remembered then that I had not. He felt I had stopped breathing and my mother had appeared to awaken me; to tell me "Not yet." It wasn't my time.

I believe he was correct. . . .

CODE BLUE

Jackie Renzulli

Jackie Renzulli worked as an independent real es
tate appraiser for fourteen years for banks and
mortgage and real estate companies in New Jersey.
She is now retired and living in the Southwest.

My mother could be difficult. She wasn't a good patient, and she often blamed me for everything that happened to her. But you only have one mother; there will
never be another one. Good, bad, or indifferent, she was
the love of my life, my stronghold.

I was a real estate appraiser living in New Jersey when
my mother died at the age of seventy-eight. I specialized
in rural areas and it was not uncommon for me to drive
hundreds of miles in a day.

My mother had been very sick for two years. The day
before Halloween of 1989 she said to me, "When you
come home tomorrow night, I want you to have a couple of drinks, cook dinner, and then come sleep in my
room."

She had a television in her room and only a twin bed, so
I found her request puzzling. "Is there something on
TV?" I asked.

"No, tomorrow night I'm going to die and I want you to
be with me."

"Mom, they don't take witches on Halloween. Cut the
bologna."

She was insistent and I finally said, "OK, fine."

Halloween night it poured. Although the rain came

down in buckets, every kid in town came out. The doorbell never stopped ringing.

Finally the trick-or-treaters all went home and I curled up in my mother's room to watch television with her. She was having trouble breathing and at midnight I finally said, "We've got to call the ambulance."

Although she insisted that she wanted to die at home, I couldn't handle what was happening, so I took her to the hospital.

Since my mom's illness began, she had been in and out of the hospital, so all the nurses, the doctors, and the EMTs knew her. After Mom was admitted that night, a nurse, who was married to a doctor, asked me to come to the lounge for a cup of coffee.

"My mother did this for two or three years," she began. "I think we should call the code."

Call the Code Blue? That's what I thought we did every time she needed to be resuscitated. But I was mistaken. In this case, "Call the code" meant that they would not resuscitate her anymore.

"It's your decision," the nurse said. "We can revive her and she'll be OK for a day or two, but she'll be back. Let her go to sleep."

This was not an easy decision for me, although I knew the nurse was right. When I finally decided to call the code, my son was so angry he stormed out of the hospital.

By 7 A.M. my mother was in a semi-coma. I was exhausted and told the nurse I was going home to take a shower and a short nap and then I'd be back.

Two and a half hours later I got a call telling me my mother had died.

I raced to the hospital and ran to my mother's room. She was still there, but ice cold. I crossed her hands and said, "Please forgive me. I knew you couldn't make it back. You were struggling too much."

Then I dropped to my knees and prayed.

A nurse I'd never seen before came in and asked, "What are you doing?"

"I'm saying a prayer for my mother."

"Why?" she said. "You weren't here when she died."

I felt terrible.

A year of depression followed. I had lived with my mother since the time I was born until her death. When you live with your mother all of your life, you tend to not stop talking to her even though she's dead. I'd come home, walk into the empty rooms, and say, "Hi, Mom, how are you?" Why? Because I couldn't stand coming in knowing she wasn't there.

Not only was my mother dead, but I felt as though I had killed her. And I sure wasn't getting any messages that she had forgiven me.

My mother had a large, multifaceted crystal that she wore all the time. After she died, I put it on a chain and draped it on the rearview mirror of my car. As I drove, it swung back and forth with the motion of the car, and the sunlight would catch its prisms.

A little over a year after her death I was out doing my job up in a rural area. My mother had grown up with horses, in a countryside very similar to what I was driving through. It was an overcast day and I was in front of a large horse farm when the crystal suddenly started flying back and forth, left to right, north to south, although the car itself was not shaking.

Shaken, I pulled off the road.

"Mom, are you here?" I asked.

The crystal began to spin.

"I'm sorry, I know you've never forgiven me for pulling the Code Blue on you."

The crystal went into a frenzy. It spun and spun although the car was still and there was no reason for it to move.

I held the crystal as I cried and cried. Somehow I knew that my mother had used her crystal, the one I'd put on my rearview mirror, to tell me that she had forgiven me.

And then I said, "Thank you, Mom."

ROMAN WARNING

Laura Day

Laura Day is a practicing intuitive who teaches all over the world. The following is an excerpt from her book, *Practical Intuition*.

I was in the front passenger seat of a car. My friend was driving us from Rome to Florence for a trade show. In Italy I often took on the habits of the Italians in not wearing my seat belt, so as the rain started methodically beating down on the roof of the car, I fell asleep without my seat belt on. I woke up to hear the screaming voice of my mother: "Put your seat belt on now!" Half asleep, I nonetheless immediately reached to fasten my seat belt. A second later I was knocked unconscious by the impact of the crash. The truck in front of us had stopped suddenly, and with the wet roads the driver of our car had been unable to brake effectively.

The driver of the truck disentangled me from the car and lifted me out. Shock was setting in as I asked if there had been any casualties and promptly forgot the answer to my question.

The next thing I remember is being on the table in the emergency room of the town hospital, with Italian voices traveling in the air above me, very confused but with a pocket of clarity when I told them that my blood pressure was normally low and that I did not think I was bleeding internally so please to wait before operating. Thank goodness, they did.

No one was severely hurt: The driver, saved by the

steering wheel, suffered only a concussion and cracked ribs, while I had sprained limbs. But without the seat belt it would have been an entirely different story.

People actually came to look at the car in the small town where the accident had happened, and a few stopped by the hospital to admire the unlikely survivors. I thought they were funny until I was discharged and went to see the car. The front was smashed like an accordion, and the top and back were buckled from the impact. I was struck by the miracle of my survival and the warning from my mother, who had died twelve years before.

A CARDINAL SIGN

Susan Claybaugh Yarina

Susan Yarina is a nurse, horsewoman, wife, mother, and for the last five years a full-time author. Her first book, *Timerider*, is a time travel romance set in 1882.

My mother and I shared a great love of nature and a rock-bottom faith in God, our Creator. Our favorite hymn was "How Great Thou Art." This hymn sings of the wonder of God as shown by His creation around us.

Our favorite tree was the aspen, our favorite flower the rose, our favorite bird the cardinal. We loved to sit and watch the birds at the feeder in her home in Phoenix, Arizona. We missed seeing the cardinal. In our home state of Indiana, where the bird is plentiful, we saw them all the time.

Mother was diagnosed with lung cancer. It shouldn't have been a surprise to me. My brother, sister, and I had begged her to quit smoking for years, but it was a shock all the same. I was literally stricken dumb. I couldn't manage anything beyond a hoarse whisper when I called and asked my doctor friends for help.

After finding cancer in her liver as well, the doctors who attended her agreed that even with chemotherapy, she would probably only have two years to live at the most.

Well, she took those two years and sometimes when we felt bravest, we would discuss what would happen after—the funeral and the dispersal of her things and funds. She would give what life advice she could, though not all at once, just little nuggets of wisdom dropped here and there.

One time when we sat at the table playing Scrabble and watching the birds, she said, "I will come back, if there is a way, and let you know that I am still caring for you. You see, I think that once you are a mother, you will always be a mother."

I choked back the tears, my throat too full to answer, and nodded. We continued to play Scrabble and watch the birds.

Time passed and Mother did as well. The grief was horrible and raw.

One morning I sat at the kitchen table, my head in my hands, and spoke silently. "Lord, I don't think I can go on. I must, though, for the sake of those who love me. I am a mother and a wife, but not very strong now. I need a sign. Please give me a sign today."

My husband tapped my shoulders and gazed into my face with a smile. With a flash of irritation at what I thought was most unsympathetic behavior, I snapped, "What? What is it?"

He just pointed outside to the bird feeder he had put up at our new home in the Superstition Mountains of Arizona. There, looking straight at me, sat a cardinal. It remained there for a full five minutes, neither eating nor moving.

My husband asked, "What are you thinking?"

"That is a sign," I replied.

He nodded. "Yes, from your mother. She is still watching out for you."

He had never heard our conversation that day. There had been no one there but my mother and myself.

The cardinal still visits. Although they are not a usual sight in this area, they are not entirely unheard of. Still, I see him every morning without fail, and whenever I fall into despair, which is rare now, I just have to look up. He will be sitting there, a blaze of red, a cardinal sign that my mother is in heaven and still watches and cares for me.

MOTHER'S FUDGE

Charlotte Fleming

Originally from West Virginia, Charlotte Fleming retired ten years ago as the office manager for the Oakland office of the Dairy Council of California. An active volunteer, her hobbies include traditional rug hooking, reading, and bridge.

Christmas was a very special time at our house when I was growing up. And one of the most special things was the food—the delicious cookies, the "popcorn balls" made with puffed wheat cereal and melted marshmallows, homemade mincemeat pie, and all the other goodies that came with the season.

Most anticipated of all, though, were the evenings when we made candy. First came the caramels that were made only at Christmas because they were so time-consuming. They took an hour to cook while "stirring constantly," and ordinarily Mother just didn't have that kind of time to spare.

We patiently waited for the candy to harden in the buttered pan so we could help with the cutting and wrapping—and sampling. Each piece had to be wrapped in a carefully cut square of waxed paper, making sure the ends were twisted tightly. My sister and I took the job seriously, but Lawrence Lee, my brother, usually lost interest when he began to feel a little queasy from all his tasting and finger licking.

Then, finally, came my favorite—the night we made fudge. Mother was famous for her peanut butter fudge.

She would stir up a batch at various times during the year: when there was a celebration, when someone needed cheering up, or just because it felt like a fudge night. We always knew what to expect when, after supper, she'd put on her flowered apron made from feed sacks and get out her big spoon and the special pan she cooked candy in.

I loved to watch her stir the rich chocolate mixture as it became too thick to fall from the spoon in twisted ribbons of luscious calories. When I grew impatient for the candy to be done, I'd often try to stick a finger into the stream of fudge as it fell back into the pan. Mother would, as I expected, crack the back of my fingers with the spoon and I'd end up with enough candy on my hand to keep me licking for at least a minute or two. Delicious! It was a game that neither she nor I ever tired of.

None of the other kids in the family seemed as interested in the actual fudge-making process as I was. Their enjoyment came after the candy was poured out on waxed paper to cool and each got a spoon to fight for whatever was left in the pan.

I tried many, many times to duplicate Mother's fudge over the years but never succeeded. I don't know how many times I went to her, nearly in tears, saying, "It just won't work! This time I ended up with chocolate syrup!" She'd patiently repeat the recipe and the step-by-step directions.

"But I did it just like that and it didn't work!" I'd say. "Why can't I make fudge like you do?"

Years passed. I married and had a daughter. Mother and Daddy moved away. I still had the old fudge recipe and periodically tried to produce even a poor facsimile of the fudge I so fondly remembered. I could duplicate her caramels, do a passable job with seaform candy, but *I couldn't make her fudge*. It became a standing joke between Mother and me. "Well, I tried again last night. This time I got a plateful of pure chocolate sugar," I'd tell her on the phone.

Then Mother became seriously ill. She had an inoperable brain tumor. The news devastated us all, but Mother's fighting spirit remained. After nearly five months in the hospital and innumerable experimental drugs, she was able to return home. She even garnered enough strength to come back to West Virginia for a visit with me and to see her ninety-four-year-old father. It was a bittersweet time for us all.

Mother's right side was paralyzed and she could walk only with the assistance of a full leg brace. Though she was in much pain, one evening she decided that it felt like a fudge night. I got out a heavy aluminum pan and added the four cups of sugar, two heaping tablespoons of cocoa, and the large can of Carnation evaporated milk her recipe called for. She watched every move I made and instructed me in every step.

"Watch how it boils up around the sides of the pan and then gradually settles down. Now test a little bit on a couple of ice cubes. Does it make a soft ball yet? Now taste it. How does it feel on your tongue? It should have some substance to it and not just dissolve away. OK, now set the pan in the sink full of ice water. And don't touch the pan until it cools. When you can comfortably hold your hand on the bottom of the pan, it's cool enough to begin stirring."

When it was finally cooled to her satisfaction, Mother asked me to set the pan on a low table in front of her wheelchair. She added two big, heaping spoonfuls of peanut butter and, with her left hand, she began stirring the rich chocolate mixture until it became too thick and creamy to run off the spoon in the well-remembered tasty twisted ribbons.

Realizing it was probably the last time I would ever have this opportunity, I stuck my finger into the stream of fudge as it fell into the pan. Mother, as I'd hoped, cracked the back of my fingers with the spoon. As I licked my fingers, tears welled up in my eyes. Delicious!

Swallowing a lump in my throat along with the candy, I asked, "Now why can't I do that?"

She looked back at me with my tears reflected in her eyes and said, "Don't worry, honey, you won't have any trouble making fudge when I'm gone, I promise."

A few days later she and my father made their final trip west across the country together. Two months later she was gone.

It was nearly a year before I could bring myself to test her promise to me. But one night, it just felt like a fudge night. I got out my pan, added the ingredients I knew by heart, and carefully followed the instructions Mother had repeated so often in the past. Her voice was almost audible. And this time it worked!

My mother's promise has held true for all these years. I've never again made chocolate syrup or pure chocolate sugar.

Mother's fudge—her final gift to me!

REACH OUT AND TOUCH SOMEONE

Donna Jenkins

 Donna Jenkins, the mother of three, is a licensed psychiatric technician. She works in a sheriff's office in California providing psychiatric care for prisoners.

I knew that he would be coming
He was expected any day
An escort for her journey
He was taking her away.

He is rarely ever welcome
Once he is in your home
You know that when he leaves
He never leaves alone.

With a stranger on a journey
Destination we don't know,
He comes and takes the ones we love
Is he friend or foe?

He came and took my mother
Right before my eyes
He seemed to bring her comfort
I could see it in her eyes.

She didn't want to leave us
She told us with a tear
But with him there to guide her
It seemed to ease her fear.

As she totally surrendered
She let him guide the way
And left me with a memory
Of that lonely day.

It hurt to see her suffer
Even more to see her leave
But he took her to a better place
That's what I believe.

My mother was a very dominant woman. As an adult she was also very controlling. She took a lot of pride in her home and it was beautiful. It had marble bathrooms, a swimming pool, and a spa, and I lived in an apartment behind it.

We were very close. Mother and I spent every day together and I'd do things with her that my sisters weren't interested in. We'd go to thrift stores, shop at dollar places, and go for walks in the mall, all things she wanted to do. We also ate dinner together. When my mother died, I didn't have a lot of guilt trips. She wasn't perfect, and neither was I, but that was OK.

My mother had survived a broken neck and several surgeries. In 1985 she was diagnosed with lymphoma (cancer of the lymph nodes), which she was able to manage along with everything else.

Mom was almost eighty when she died. She'd had two face-lifts and tummy tucks, and four husbands, all younger than her except for my father. She never really took to aging and I always knew she would die when she got frail.

When she was diagnosed with lung cancer, the doctor gave her three months to live. Right after that she began having strokes. She was a very strong-willed woman and I really think she was willing herself to die. Within three days of the diagnosis, she did just that.

After the strokes she couldn't speak. We kept her at home. The night before she died, I climbed in bed with her, and it was as if she was waiting for something.

Mom had taken care of all her funeral plans except for one detail. She had never bought a casket. The next day, June 1, 1996, my sister and I bought one and came home and told her. She was failing fast and we called in a priest (although she no longer went to church) who gave her the last rites. Then we fed her broth, bathed her, changed her, and combed her hair. Finally, my sister and I told her that it was all right for her to leave. But even after the family all came, she still seemed to be waiting for something.

My mom's timing was impeccable. She waited until we got all of the family members together, and as we gathered around her bed, in the house she loved, holding her hands, she died. It was five minutes to eight and her death was followed by the most beautiful sunset I'd ever seen.

After our mother's death my sister and I took a walk through the neighborhood. It was strange, but we felt as though we could breathe and everything was really OK because she had been suffering so much. We didn't cry right away.

Mom knew a lot of people in her neighborhood and many of them stopped us that night and asked, "How's your mom?" When we said that she'd just passed away they looked at us like we were crazy.

After her death, I asked every day in my thoughts, "Mom, are you all right?"

My mother worried about me. Out of her four girls, I was the only one who did not own my own home. I had lost my house and security in a divorce a few years earlier and was having a very difficult time starting over. Mom had mentioned several times her desire to leave me her house, because I didn't have one and because I was always there for her. At the same time, she feared I might not be able to afford the upkeep. I felt it would not be fair to my sisters. Once mother was gone, all we would have was each other. Although we were not extremely close, we never fought and were always happy when we got together.

Mom knew I wanted the house. I knew she worried about me and wanted me to have it, but I also knew how important my sisters were to me, and the trouble my keeping it would cause was not worth it to me.

Her house had been listed and on the market for a year. I had been in an accident and was expecting a settlement and was going to buy a home. Although hers was for sale, I couldn't afford it or the maintenance it required. No one could understand why Mom's house didn't sell. People looked at it, but there were no offers. The Realtors were stunned. The house was beautiful, the price was right, why didn't it sell?

My mother always worried about me and I somehow knew that she was not going to release that house until my new husband and I had a home. We found a house we liked, put in an offer, and almost the minute our offer was accepted, my mother's house sold. It was like she could finally let go of hers. The people who bought it were just like her; they didn't change a thing in her home.

During the time her home was on the market, I would go by and check on the house and pool. We'd had an estate sale and the house was practically empty, other than a couch and a chair that I was going to move to my new house. I went over to pick up the furniture one day, and every light in the house was on. I realized I didn't have my keys, so I went back to my house to get them. When I returned to my mom's house, all the lights were off.

Another time, I went in her house and started checking things out, and while I was in the bathroom, I heard the telephone ring. I started down the hall to the bedroom and then realized that there was no telephone there. Then I went to the kitchen to get the wall phone before I remembered that there was no phone there. In fact, there were no phones at all in the house.

I thought it was really weird that the phones were ringing when there weren't any there. I wasn't scared; I just thought it strange. When I went home and told my family, they said, "You're crazy."

Two weeks later I took my ten-year-old over to Mom's house with me. I was standing outside talking to a neighbor when my son came tearing out of the house. He was shaking, out of breath, and couldn't talk. He didn't need to. The neighbor and I could hear the telephone ringing from deep inside my mother's house.

The funny thing is, when Mom was alive, she wanted us to call every day.

Today I feel my mother is with me all the time. I have to be strong and she helps me. She was always there for her family and me. She was strong and knew just what to do. Now I find myself having to do the same for my adult children and I'm doing it.

Of course, she's guiding me along.

BUNNY HOP

Eileen Dudley

Eileen Dudley, sixty-three, is a retired community services worker. Born and raised in Chicago, she is a master gardener with a university and county extension program. Eileen makes handcrafted soap that she sells through her local art museum and botanical garden.

My friend Lori and I walked out of the hospital. My mother had died at 10:35 P.M. and it was now after midnight. It was a warm night in late June, and I could see a few stars. We talked a little, wept, and hugged each other, and then I headed home to a house that would be forever empty of my mother.

I drove through dark and quiet streets in this little town in Ohio my mother had lived in for nearly fifty years. As I turned slowly into the driveway, I saw a cottontail rabbit sitting quietly right in the middle of it. As I slowly pulled up, the rabbit moved very slowly off the driveway onto the grass. Then it turned around and faced me.

I shut off the engine, collected Mom's few things from her last trip to the hospital, and got out of the car. The rabbit still sat there quietly and calmly watching me, no more than six feet away. We stood looking at each other for a long minute. And then it hit me. It was my mother telling me that she was all right. Then I said, "Momma, you got back home before I did."

The Western mind always wants to rationalize everything. If you ask me how I knew that the rabbit was my mother, all I can say is that I *just knew*. I sat with my mother while she was dying for five days, and during this time I slept very little. My mind was probably in an altered state. An hour earlier I had watched my mother draw her last breath, and when I saw that little cottontail, I just *knew* it was my mother.

As I let myself into the house the rabbit still sat quietly, watching me. I shut the door.

I slept a deep, long sleep that night. The next day I awoke to sunshine and started sorting through years of accumulation of my mother's modest possessions. Through the long hours of sorting and packing, from time to time I found things that had rabbits on them. A key ring with a Canadian coin that had an engraving on one side. A tiny toy rabbit I had given my mother years and years before, which I had forgotten all about. A small hand towel with a rabbit embroidered on it. I never knew how fond my mother was of rabbits until I sorted through her things.

When I got back home days later, I spent three evenings walking with a friend in a lovely secluded canyon. Each evening at different times during the walk a rabbit appeared, streaked across our path, and ran beside us for a few feet before disappearing off into the bush. It was just one rabbit, once each evening.

And each time I said, "Hi, Mom. I know you're checking up on me," or, "Hi, Mom. I miss you badly, but I'm doing all right."

I have walked in the canyon a few times after that. But I have not seen a rabbit since.

THE RED RIBBON

Anita González

Along with her husband, Danny, Anita González has successfully raised three children. She is still fighting the demons of her past. Two years ago, at the age of forty-three, she tried to end the pain with a single gunshot to her heart. Today she's happy she didn't succeed.

On July 25, 1993, the life of my mother was taken in a split second. A second that seemed to go on forever. As I kissed her tears away, I watched my mother helplessly take her last breath. The Angel of Death reached out his hand and her spirit was set free, leaving me alone to sing her favorite hymns, starting with "I Come to the Garden Alone."

I had a difficult time accepting my mother's death, because she gave me one whole year of close friendship before she died. This was especially important to me for a number of reasons, which I shall soon explain.

My mother tried very hard to abort me forty-two years ago. Unhappy at being pregnant, she took many pills and drank heavily. Probably because of that, my mother's pregnancy was difficult.

I was the youngest of five children, and when they brought me home from the hospital, my oldest sister, who was then thirteen, said, "Mommy, you don't want that baby, but she's so beautiful."

Mom broke down and cried and said, "No, I don't want her."

I was always aware of how unwanted I was. There were years and years of emotional and physical abuse. As a small child, I was beaten and given whiskey every night before I went to bed. My mother did whatever else she could to get back at me for making her life miserable.

She was also very mistreated by my father emotionally, and she took it out on us kids. I still bear scars on my head from her bashings, and burns on my arms, which were warnings to stay out of her kitchen. Those aren't the only scars I have.

I did everything I could to please my mom. If she said, "Jump," I jumped. If she said, "Get the hell out of my house," I did.

I've gone through years of therapy and still have trouble accepting myself. I've also tried to commit suicide several times.

I wasn't a bad kid, but I did ditch school. We were living in Minnesota and I remember being too ashamed to go to class. I knew I was stupid. After all, hadn't I been told that all of my life? And wearing my brother's hand-me-downs was embarrassing, since all of the other girls were in school uniforms. I discovered a neighbor's tree house and I'd climb up there and freeze rather than go to school. To this day, I don't like heights.

I tried to sneak out of the house a couple of times, and my mother caught me. She nailed the windows shut and locked me in my room for weeks. During most of that time I went without food. The only time I was let out was when my mother was either in the regular hospital for drinking or in a psychiatric ward.

My father also participated in my abuse. The last time it happened was when I was seventeen. They put a leather strap around me and beat me. Yet I would not drop a tear. I don't know what gave me the strength, but I broke out of the straps and ran.

In those days, bamboo flip-flop sandals were very popular, and I was wearing a pair when I ran away from home. They flew off my feet and I ran for miles and miles, finally ending up next to an interstate highway. I found a telephone and called the cops, asking them to come pick me up, but then I chickened out and began running again.

I spent the next two weeks running, stealing what clothes I needed from clotheslines and sleeping in open flatbed trucks when I could find them. Finally the investigators caught up with me. As an incorrigible runaway I was brought into Juvenile Detention, where I stayed for a week. That gave me a lot of time to come up with a plan. After I explained my situation to the juvenile court judge, he signed papers that granted permission for me and my boyfriend, who was also underage, to get married.

Two weeks later, armed with the judge's authorization, we eloped.

I wrote my parents a letter and told them that I loved them and that I had forgiven them for everything they had done to me. My mother said, "You're crazy, absolutely crazy. We don't love you and there is no reason for you to love us."

The year before my mother died (neither one of us knew she was sick then), I went over to her house and said, "One of these days, Mom, will you please tell me I'm not crazy or stupid? Will you tell me exactly what happened? If you tell me you didn't want me, I can accept that."

That's when she finally told me the truth. She had just come home from the hospital, weak and exhausted from heart trouble, when my father raped her. That's how I was conceived, through a spousal rape.

She then told me that I was not crazy, I wasn't stupid or fat (I'm five feet ten and 130 pounds), and that she did love me.

And that's when we finally became friends. Although Mom was close to being agoraphobic, we started doing things. We'd go shopping, have a beer or a cigarette together, and talk. We didn't touch though. I don't like to be touched, probably because I never was as a child. It still feels foreign to me.

Shortly before my mother died, one of my sisters and I were with her. Mom said, "I'm so jealous of you girls. You can put your hair in a ponytail. Will you please put this red ribbon in my hair?"

She didn't have much hair at that time, but somehow we managed to tie the ribbon in it.

Twenty years to the day that I left her to get married, my mother left me.

When I came home from the hospital the day she died, the red ribbon was waiting for me on my kitchen counter.

I went crazy and asked my husband and all three of my kids, "Where did that ribbon come from? Did you put it there?"

One of the kids said, "Mom, we don't know. It looks like something Grandma would wear."

There was no explanation. Exhausted from grief, I fell asleep. When I woke up, I saw Mom walking away, holding the hand of Jesus on the right-hand side of God. Suddenly I knew she went to the right place, that she wasn't doomed to be damned.

Over the years, I have also been able to smell my mother. Perfume drives me crazy and makes me sick, but my mother always wore a fragrance that I loved. Whenever she is near, I can still smell it.

Just a week ago my son and husband suddenly asked me, "Do you smell that?" They were smelling her perfume.

"Mom, don't you smell it?" my son asked again.

I didn't, so I said no, but then, finally, I smelled her.

My son was amazed. "Mom," he confessed, "you're not crazy, you really did smell her all those other times, she's really here."

My brother came over two days ago after hearing about the Feathers Project. He gave me a paper and said, "There's this lady who's writing a book and I think you might want to talk to her." I took the paper and started crying.

After he left, still crying I went into my bedroom. There on the bed was the red ribbon we had put in Mom's hair.

I have no idea how it got there, as I keep it in a chest in another room and there was no one else in the house.

MOTHER'S MESSENGER

Eleanor Lewis

Eleanor Lewis, now retired, did research in the Navy as a Wave during World War II. Her interest thus piqued, she went on to explore organic and inorganic chemistry and was involved in medical research. Eleanor is also a former elementary school teacher.

In January of 1963, I was returning from visiting my brother and his family in Los Angeles. I had promised my parents to stop by their place in Torrance before I returned to my own home in Long Beach. As I drove I thought about that promise. I was tired and I really wanted to go home. When the cutoff to the Harbor Freeway, which would take me to Torrance, approached, I suddenly decided to go home to Long Beach. I would see my parents later in the week.

I never saw my father alive again. He died suddenly the next day.

In January of 1986, I went on a tour of Europe. When I returned the following month, I found my mother was very ill.

I immediately went to Mother's home to stay with her. The day after my arrival, my sister relieved me at about 11 A.M. When I came back later that afternoon I was informed by my brother that our mother had died.

The date was February 10, 1986.

Almost a year later, on Sunday, February 9, 1987, I went

to the Inglewood Park Cemetery mausoleum to take care of the graves of my mother, father, paternal grandmother, and my brother Jerry, along with those of my Uncle Ralph and Aunt Mariane. The first four were in a unit easily accessible from the entrance of the building.

To find my aunt's and uncle's resting places, I had to go down a corridor of wall graves where they had full-length caskets and make a few turns. I had never been to the mausoleum on a Sunday before. Unlike my previous visits, there was no sound except for the recorded music. There were no other visitors, no workmen going in and out, no sound of traffic or of doors opening and closing. It was weird.

Suddenly all I wanted to do was to get out of there as soon as possible, so I hurried up and cleaned the faces of the various repositories and put new flowers in the holders. With a feeling of relief, I was exiting toward the main entrance when I felt a force behind me.

It was like a strong compressed wind pushing me toward the door. There was no feeling of a breeze on either side of me, only a steady push on my back.

At this late date I do not know whether I turned around, looked over my shoulder, or simply instinctively knew that it was my mother who was generating the force.

Mother did not look as she did when she had died the year before at ninety-two. She was about twenty-five to thirty years younger. Except for a large weight loss during a two-year illness, my mother had always been heavy during her adult years. That is how I saw her. She wore an outfit I remembered well, for she had designed it—a yellow flowered top with a medium-brown loose skirt. I remembered the clothing because it had been hanging in the closet and after her death we had washed and ironed it and sent it to Goodwill.

My mother was shoving me toward the exit, telling me, without speaking, to hurry.

Ever since I was a child I had thought my mother had often read my thoughts. As an adult I rationalized that all children probably felt that way because adults know so much more than they do that adults can probably anticipate certain childish actions.

However, a few years before she died, my mother was annoyed or frustrated by some situation I no longer recall. Suddenly she broke off from what she had been saying, and said angrily, "Sometimes I can read minds. It's a gift I never wanted and I don't see why I had to have it." I was so startled at the time that I didn't ask her to explain.

But that day in February, I knew why my mother was pushing me out of the mausoleum. The graves could wait, but her best friend was in trouble and needed me.

My next stop after the cemetery was to be Irene Klein's home in Carson, California. I understood from my mother that I was to hurry there and not change my plans.

In retrospect, perhaps my quickly heeding my mother's instructions stemmed from my not having done so twenty-four years earlier when my father had died and I had gone on to Long Beach.

Earlier, Irene and I had talked about my moving in with her. I was to help clean out her deceased husband's bedroom and make it habitable for a possible home health aide. Irene was in her late eighties and the emphysema that had made her an invalid for the last twenty years was worsening.

When I arrived that afternoon, I found her in bed, a luxury I had never known her to allow herself before. She was turned on her right side, facing the edge of the bed, with her beloved longhaired cat snuggled up to her head. At her request I evicted it to the front part of the house.

Irene's breathing was bad and the cat was dangerously impeding it.

She wanted a fresh fruit salad and gave me money to buy a supply of food, which I did. When I returned from the store, she was no longer interested in eating; she just wanted to rest.

I needed to return home, so I talked to one of Irene's neighbors, who promised to call Irene's sister in San Diego.

During the time I was there that evening, she said something I've never forgotten. You see, Irene was dying from emphysema, brought on by smoking two to three packs of cigarettes a day. The subject of smoking came up and Irene said fiercely, "I don't regret a single cigarette. I loved every moment of smoking." Then she paused, smiled, and said, "Didn't we think we were sophisticated with our cigarettes?"

I suspect that without my visiting her, Irene would have died alone, probably on the first anniversary of my mother's death, February 10, helped along by her beloved cat.

She was a proud, stubborn individual who would not have asked for help.

My mother would have asked for help, nay screamed for it, and when my mother screamed, all of the children and most of the neighbors would come running. I think one of the reasons my mother returned and directed earth's affairs was so her old friend would not have to go through what she did when she died.

At the time of my mother's illness, I was working in the Miami University School of Medicine emergency services heart program under the auspices of the anesthesiology department. I gained a lot of medical knowledge, understood patients' charts, and knew something about illness and death. My sister did not and was uneasy with my mother's illness.

She called 911 when my mother died. I would not have. I never asked but know what could have happened—CPR, a trip to the ER with shouting, possibly even IVs inserted, useless though they might be. It was far too late when I arrived to tell what procedures had been started. Perhaps Mother's intervention was to save her friend from a similar fate.

When Irene's sister came up two days after my visit, she got her admitted to Kaiser Permanente Hospital.

I was going to see her that night after work, but my car acted up. I called the hospital, talked to Irene's nurse, told her my problem, and asked her to give my friend my love. She died the next day, Lincoln's birthday, February 12.

Thinking about all this, it came to me that mother and Irene were like two primitive goddesses and I was like Iris, the messenger of the gods.

There are worse things to be in this life than your mother's messenger.

MOONLIGHT SONATA

Elsa Paine Mulhern

After a long career as a corporate attorney, Elsa immersed herself in Republican politics and the arts, particularly theater. On her eighty-ninth birthday she rode the rapids on a wild Oregon river. Shortly before her death at the age of ninety-one, she underwrote a production of *Wit*, a play about meeting mortality with grace and honor.

My mother died when I was only five years old, so I am not sure how much of my memory of her is truly memory and how much is what others told me. I know her also as she appears in the beautiful portraits of her that hang in my home. She was a gentle and lovely person, an accomplished pianist, and a devoted mother to my sister and me. My sister inherited her talent for music, but I inherited only her love of it.

She appears to me often in my dreams, and at times these are daydreams, when I think of her with regret at not having known her all the years of my growing up and my adulthood.

I have never mentioned this before, but after my husband died, when all the family members had left and I was quite alone, I heard the "Moonlight Sonata" being played on a piano. I have no piano in my home. Could it have been my mother comforting me?

CARDIAC ATTEST

Lisa Slayton Loveland

Lisa Slayton Loveland is a licensed practical nurse with a critical-care nursing specialty. She is currently working in cancer prevention studies at the Arizona Cancer Center. Lisa, forty-eight, lives with her husband and dog in Tucson, Arizona.

I was the only daughter in my family and the last born. My mother and I were very close. We were best friends from the time I was a youngster through my adult years. We looked alike, were the same size, shared clothes, had the same spirit, and even took vacations together. She used to call me Sister or Sissy as a nickname, and as a young teen I would get embarrassed. As I got older I found it endearing. Even my dad would call me Sissy long after Mother had died.

My mother was a nurse and I grew up to also be a nurse. There really was a link between us.

Mother had rheumatic heart disease, leaving her with bad heart valves. She had her first open heart surgery when I was five. Her second came when I was twelve.

I was twenty-one and had just graduated from nursing school in 1972 when Mother went to Lackland Air Force Base in San Antonio for her third open heart surgery. I was working in a coronary care unit in Dayton, Ohio, and I flew down to Texas to be with her. Three days after her operation she was out of the ICU, so I left. I was then stunned when my father called me and said that Mother had died suddenly.

I was devastated that I didn't get to say good-bye to her.

My father had her cremated in Texas, so when she got home all we had was cremains to mourn to.

My mother was forty-six when she died. She was twenty one when she lost her own mother, the same age I was when I lost her.

I was still struggling with my grief several weeks after she died. People would say, "Why don't you take some time off?" and I'd reply that I needed to be doing something.

One day I was really upset and working in the coronary care unit when a man I'd never seen before had a coronary arrest. The flat line on his EKG indicated that his heart had stopped. A Code Blue was called and we were able to bring him back. Arrangements were being made to move him to a more intensive area of the unit.

There were just the two of us—he and I—in the room when he asked me to come over and sit next to him. He knew only my name, nothing else about me. As I sat on the bed, he took my hand. Then he looked at me. "I have something to tell you," he said. "I've just seen your mother and she told me to tell you that she's OK and not to be sad. She loves you."

Right after he told me this, he went flat-line.

We coded him again, but couldn't bring him back.

I was so busy trying to resuscitate him that the impact of the experience didn't hit me until we stopped the code. Then I felt as though I was ready to faint.

"Your color is gone," another nurse said. "You look like you've seen a ghost."

"I think I have," I replied.

I truly believe that my mother used this dying heart patient to send a message to me.

After that I went to an Elisabeth Kübler-Ross seminar,

and that helped put things in perspective. I was convinced this message from my mother was meant only for me.

A short time later I learned that my mother had given me an even greater gift.

I went to work nights in the same coronary care unit. We'd get reports on the patients at the change of shift, and I found myself somehow knowing when a certain patient was going to die.

I'd float between my own unit and Pediatric ICU. I'd see a light, a brightness around the children who were going to die. I think it was because they were so innocent. In the adult unit it was just a feeling I had.

I found myself saying to the people I was working with, "Mrs. Smith is going to die today between two and three."

People started calling me the Kiss of Death. It didn't bother me, because I knew that I was given the gift of knowing when they were going to die so that if their families weren't going to be there, I could be with them. If they were there, then I could prepare them.

I think this was definitely a gift from my mother, because she was a very, very good nurse. Or maybe it was a gift from God, given to me after my mother's death. Either way, it was meant for the good.

One woman was in a coma for six weeks. We didn't expect her to ever come out of it, but she awakened one day when I was with her. She told me she saw her mother. The patient had such an angelic look, a contentment about her. She asked me to brush her hair because that was what her mother would do. I was doing just that when she died.

Others wouldn't wake up, but they would die while I was with them. I'd tell them, "It's OK, you can go now."

This gift has followed me all the years since 1972. It still happens.

Most recently I was working in a university hospital cardiac ICU with heart transplant patients. A friend's grandfather—we called him Bampa—had had a stroke and had been in another hospital for several weeks.

I was working nights and something woke me up at four in the afternoon (which is like 2 A.M. for day people). I knew that I had to go to Bampa's room. I drove to the hospital and the nurse on duty told me the family had just left. I went to his room, sat by his side, and whispered, "It's OK, you can go now." Then I kissed him and he died.

Several years ago Bampa's daughter got lung cancer. She had done well with her chemotherapy. While the tumor was gone, her lungs were inflamed. Hers was clearly a case of "If the cancer doesn't kill you, the treatment will."

I went to visit her one night and got that feeling again, so I called her husband and the rest of the family. I didn't want to alarm them, so I said, "I don't know why, but we need to be in her room at six-thirty tomorrow morning when the doctor comes in." We were all there at the appointed time and she died fifteen minutes later. It was very peaceful and everyone got to say good-bye. Her husband told me, "I can't thank you enough for having us be here."

At the end of May, I lost my father. He was in the late stages of lung disease and I had just moved him from Medford, Oregon, to my home. I was able to take a leave of absence to be with my dad and take care of him.

He wasn't doing well. He'd wake up and see my mother, who of course had died years earlier.

I feel that when people are dying or very, very ill, there's something that opens up that isn't usually there because it's restricted by consciousness. When the brain is freed, you're like a child again and those things can come in again. That's why the dying and the young can see and feel those people who are no longer on earth. And that's what my father was doing.

"I don't want to die in your bed," my father said. "I don't want your memory of me to be my dying in your and your husband's bed."

I acquiesced to his wishes and called the hospice. They came out, assessed him, and asked if I knew he was dying. Of course I did.

My father went into the hospice thirty-six hours before his death. Once he was in there, I found that I could just be a daughter again. I was no longer the nurse/caretaker.

I spent the day with him. He was seeing my mother a lot now. When I got the call the next morning, I knew to go.

"Go with Mother," I told him when I got there. "There's no reason to stay anymore, just go."

The nurse asked me if there was something else he needed to do.

While my brother had already said his good-byes, I thought maybe my father needed to hear him just one more time. I reached my brother in Tacoma and said, "Say good-bye to Dad so he can hear you again."

After my brother said good-bye, I lay with my father and held him. "It's OK, you can go now," I said and then he stopped breathing.

Now that I'm no longer working in ICU, I don't have the feelings as much as I did.

But I have no doubt that the gift from my mother is still there.

MOTHER'S LILIES

Brooke Franko

Brooke Franko, fifty-three, grew up in Pennsylvania. A psychiatric nurse, she is also an avid gardener.

We lived in a little town called McKeesport, Pennsylvania, outside of Pittsburgh. While my mom and I had trouble during my teenage years, after I got married and started a family, we became much closer and talked almost every day on the phone.

My mother died very suddenly. I was in nursing school at the time, and I got a telephone call one morning saying that she had died in her sleep. She had had a heart valve repair sometime earlier, and the valve was not a good one. When the doctors suggested replacing it, Mother refused, saying that one heart operation was enough for anyone.

My mother knew that I was very much into gardening and flowers. In my yard there were two plants that I couldn't identify that came up every spring. No one else ever recognized the plants either. But they were always healthy with lots of leaves. They had something else in common: Neither ever bloomed.

After my mom died in February of 1980, the very next spring both plants came up and then died back as they usually did. Then, late in the summer, one of them shot up a stalk that had pink flowers on it. This was the first time either plant had ever bloomed! More eager than ever to identify the plant, I continued searching for its name. When I finally identified it, I knew right away that my mother was sending me this flower. What was it? A Resurrection Lily.

It came up the next summer, and again only one of the two plants bloomed.

It was blooming for the third time one Sunday in August of 1982. I was working the night shift and slept several hours and awoke at noon. I had a strong urge to go visit my father, so I went to his house and we sat around and talked for some time before I returned home.

That afternoon a friend called and asked me to go out for coffee. My husband and older son were out, but I felt confident in leaving my eleven-year-old home alone as long as it was daylight. I gave him strict orders to stay inside the house.

As the afternoon wore on, I noticed that it was getting dark, and I told my friend, "I need to go home since I don't want Dane alone at night." As I drove up the back alley I found my son riding his bike.

"You know you aren't supposed to be out here—you're supposed to be in the house," I chastised him.

"I'm afraid to go inside," he said. "The lights are going on and off in my bedroom."

He refused to go in with me and I walked all through the house and didn't find anything. As I came downstairs, the basement door squeaked and then opened. I knew if there was anyone in the house that they were in the basement, so I quickly closed and locked the door and then called my father.

He came over immediately and checked things out. Once he was convinced that there was no one there, he walked outside and then he fell over dead on my porch with a heart attack.

I couldn't get out the front door because he was lying against it. I had to use the back door and run around the house to the porch. When I finally got to him, I began

CPR. Suddenly I had a strong feeling and it was as though my mother was saying, "Stop it! Leave him alone! This is his time." This was, of course, contrary to all of my teachings. As a nurse you only stop CPR when a doctor tells you to, when someone relieves you, or when you are too exhausted to continue. Still, the feelings were too strong and I listened to them, stopped my rescue attempts, and my father died.

When I looked up at the house, the lights were again coming on, then off. I really feel that my mother had a large part in how my father died. I think she did not want us to find him dead in his house, knowing that it might have been several days before we found him. She did the lights so I'd call him and he would come over.

The year after my father's death the blooming Resurrection Lily, the one that I'd come to think of as a gift from my mother, didn't bloom. Strangely enough, that summer the second one did for the first time.

When my sister visited, I said, "The plant from Mother didn't bloom this year, but this one did and I think it's Daddy's."

My sister went outside to look at the lily and then quickly came back in. "I think you need to look at the plant," she said.

On closer inspection I saw that there were actually two stalks on the Resurrection Lily blooming side by side.

After that year, neither plant ever bloomed again. In fact, they died out completely.

SING AND SNORE ERNIE

Mary Dickinson

Mary Dickinson, thirty-eight, is an education coordinator for a large university. A softball mom, her hobbies include reading, hiking, and anything to do with the outdoors.

It was difficult growing up with six girls in my family. We were all within nine years of each other—the oldest is now forty-three, the youngest thirty-four. The competition for our parents' attention was keen. My mother loved her privacy and alone time for herself. We didn't have a lot of one-on-one time with her as children.

My sisters and I weren't really friends with our mother. Mommy didn't want that kind of relationship. She wasn't the kind of mother who played games with you or became a Girl Scout troop leader or soccer mom. As we grew up, we didn't have lunch or shopping dates. We didn't call each other on the phone to gossip. As a devoted ex-nun, my mother spent her "kid time" with us at church. Except for a strong desire to have the Catholic religion in our lives, she wasn't much involved in planning our weddings or any other celebrations. Her role as matriarch meant that she managed her family in such a way that her authority was respected and deserved.

Mommy was very intelligent. Highly educated, she was the kind of person who did crossword puzzles with a pen. She became politically involved in issues that affected her family and community. An artist and a counselor, she liked to paint, read, write, and watch movies. Suffering from chronic depression, basically she was a recluse. That obviously affected how we grew up and our relationships with her.

Having been diagnosed with adult-onset diabetes for over twenty years, the last five years of her life my mother developed diabetic neuralgia. This is basically a disease of the nerves. With hers permanently damaged, she was in constant pain, moaning and groaning in anguish. It was heart wrenching for us to see her suffering. During the last year of her life she was finally given a narcotic patch to wear, which helped relieve the pain. She improved, but was on continual narcotic medication.

My mother died of a heart attack last February, at the age of seventy-two. While she'd had no history of heart disease, we thought that the strong narcotic drug that she was taking affected her awareness of chest pains. Perhaps the drug patch dulled her discomfort. A smoker for sixty years, she came home from church that Sunday and probably had a cigarette on the way home. Once inside the house, she sat down and had a heart attack.

My dad was home sick that day, which was out of the ordinary since he usually went to a Presbyterian church every Sunday. My mother called to him from the other room, and he took her immediately to the hospital.

She was conscious for about another twenty-four hours and died at dawn the next morning.

My daughter Emily was five when Mommy died. The year before, I had bought a Sing and Snore Ernie doll for her. These dolls were very popular that Christmas. In fact, lotteries were held for them.

The Christmas before my mother's death I decided to give my daughter the doll. She was four and perhaps a little old for the doll, so she didn't really play with it much. Ernie said three or four things. He'd snore like he was sleeping. If you picked him up and held him, he'd say, "I feel great," because he'd just gotten up from his nap. He also sang "Twinkle, Twinkle, Little Star." But Emily didn't play with him. She was more interested in her Barbie dolls, and Ernie just sat around the house.

About three weeks after my mom died, I was having a dream. My five sisters and I were all going to fly away with Mom on a trip. She was going to be the pilot. This was a small ten-passenger plane and we were all standing outside ready to board. I think we were going to Paris for the weekend! I was talking with my sisters about a new purse I had purchased for the journey, when I turned to my mom and asked, "Are you feeling OK? Because you just had a heart attack and I don't know if you're ready to fly this airplane." She said, "I feel great."

I woke up hearing, "I feel great. I feel great. I feel great." I thought, What is that? Then I heard it again. "I feel great. I feel great. I feel great." I was scared because I thought a stranger was in the house. When I called out to my husband, he didn't wake up. And the voice was still saying off and on, "I feel great."

Creeping around the quiet, dark house, I finally tracked down the noise. It was Sing and Snore Ernie. I went into the family room grumbling, "Shut up, doll. This is too freaky."

When I found him, he was lying down, although up until then, he never said "I feel great" unless he was picked up or sitting up. Yet here he was lying down and he wouldn't shut up.

The doll had been sitting—silently—on the table for two months, untouched by my daughter.

When I told my sisters about my experience, they wanted Mommy to come talk to them too.

It left me wondering, Why would my mom tell me she feels great? She's out of her body and she's gone to heaven. She was in so much pain before she died, and while I was delighted to hear "I feel great," why had I received this wondrous message?

Then I figured it out.

Occasionally I'd gone to see psychics. I would get a reading or have the tarot cards read. Right before my mother died, I'd told her about a psychic reading I'd had done. My mom did not believe in psychics. She thought it was all a bunch of garbage. She'd frequently ask me, "Why do you waste your money on that?" But I'd still share my experiences with her.

I think that's the reason she might have come to me with that message that night. She knew that I believed in the ability of another world or realm. She knew that if she gave me that message, I would definitely believe in it.

And I do.

A GIFT IN THE MIDDLE OF THE ROAD

Nancy Coomer

Nancy Coomer, fifty, is a trial lawyer. The mother of two boys, she enjoys gardening and is a reluctant ranch hand.

While Carena Kurth was not actually Nancy's mother, they had a very special relationship akin to that of mother/daughter. As Nancy says, "The Kurths were an old couple, at least twenty-five years older than our parents, living up on the hill above us, and the rest of us were all in our early twenties."

That friendship evolved into a very close family relationship. This is Nancy's story. . . .

We were caretaking an old ranch in the Nevada desert when Carena Kurth came into my life. She and her husband, Rudolph Friend Kurth, had been married for over fifty years. He worked as a machinist and she took in boarders in their house, which was located right in the center of downtown Los Angeles. After saving their money, they retired to a tiny travel trailer on one of the forty-acre lots that shysters sell in the desert, and they became our neighbors.

They had no water, but they found a spring over a mile away. Undaunted, they bought a backhoe and dug a huge ditch and pipeline. Even before they had a spring, they grew a little orchard that they watered by hand with trucked-in water. They knew they were planting trees that they wouldn't see mature, but they didn't care. In fact, they rather liked the idea. They were both great human beings. In that tiny eight-foot travel trailer, Carena would put together dinners like you wouldn't believe.

But it all changed when Friend got sick with cancer. It happened very quickly. He went into the hospital, was diagnosed, and never came home. Carena would stay at the hospital with him in Salt Lake City, but she couldn't stay all the time. Sometimes she just needed to get out on the mountain, where she could see for a million miles.

My husband, Danny, and I had a little struggling garden that specialized in miniature vegetables. One day Carena and I were out on the mountain and she said, "Let's pickle your tiny little beets."

I had never canned before. But we dug in and pickled them. I was worried because the jars didn't seal.

"Don't worry," Carena said. "They'll seal themselves by tomorrow."

She was right. I heard the jars popping all night.

Friend died a short time later.

During their L.A. days, Friend and Carena had bought cemetery plots in Forest Lawn, and so we had to take Carena to Hollywood to bury Friend. It was quite a sight, all of these young people in their twenties—there were six or seven of us—descending on Forest Lawn with this elderly lady.

Friend died in September. During his illness Carena didn't want to worry anyone with her failing health. But after he died, she realized that she really needed some help.

During the time we were friends with Friend and Carena, we were also building on forty acres we had bought. Since we had been living on the mountain for several years before the land was carved up for sale, we knew what we were buying. We had two springs, aspens, junipers, cedars, all bought for eight thousand dollars. We were camping up there in a van while we were building a house, so we didn't have the facilities to have Carena come live with us.

One day, my friend Katie and I went, unannounced, to see the lawyer who represented the Church of the Latter Day Saints, which owned a prefab ranch house in the valley. We thought it was luxurious with its radiant heat and running water. When we explained that we wanted a place so that an elderly, recently widowed woman could come to live with us, the lawyer immediately gave us the use of the ranch house, although he had never seen it before and we weren't even members of the church.

A short time later after we moved into the ranch house, Carena was diagnosed with lung cancer.

We'd take her 120 miles into Salt Lake City for her doctor's appointments. Soon she and I began fussing with each other because the doctor was telling her to do certain things, but what did she care? She'd lost her husband and she didn't care if she stayed on the planet.

I got it into my head that she needed someone to want her to live. I'd nag her with advice like, "Don't smoke, take your medicine," things like that. Sometimes we would get into pitched battles. Toward the end she got kind of delirious and would do things like waking up in the night and trying to smoke a Kleenex. I always knew when she was awake, and would sit with her to make sure she didn't accidentally do something that would hurt us.

We continued fussing with one another until three days before she died, when both of us hit the same level of understanding at the same time. I started saying things like, "I've made you this special breakfast, but you don't have to eat it." She'd reply, "I'm really not hungry, but let me try."

One morning we went to awaken her and realized that she couldn't wake up.

We put her in the car and took her to the hospital in Salt Lake City. There the doctors told us, "She's in a coma. Go home, take care of what you need to do, and then come back."

We had jobs that we needed to go do, so we couldn't stay and needed to go home. During this time I kept wondering where she was while she was in her coma. Was she out of body? Was she with us? Or with Friend? Was she dropped in an invisible waiting room somewhere reading outdated magazines?

Before we were able to get back to Salt Lake City, friends drove out to the ranch to tell us that Carena had died.

I remember that winter as having horrible smells—the hospital smell, Carena's smell, her room—hot, cooped-up, unhealthy smells. But the day she died was the first day of spring and it was beautiful and you could smell the sagebrush.

I took a walk in the desert, walking around with what she knew and loved, the smell of the sagebrush, the light of the mountains, and then I started thinking to her. I kept thinking, *If I made a mistake fighting for you so hard to make you stay with us, I'm really sorry. What should I have done? Did I do the right thing?* A short time later, I said, "Carena, I'm sorry you're gone, but send me a sign that everything's OK."

Not two minutes later I was walking down a dirt road traveled by no more than three to four cars a week. Suddenly I saw, in the middle of the road where it should not have been, a perfectly whole, uncracked, unblemished, faded blue mason jar. Anyone in a car would have seen it and picked it up, or missed seeing it and run it over. Yet it was in perfect condition.

I knew it was my sign. There couldn't be any question about it. And I knew that whatever I had done to make her passing more difficult was forgiven, and that she loved me for trying.

I have only a few of Carena's personal belongings by which to remember her, but the items I have would be precious, even in a larger collection. I have her pearls—a graduated string of almost perfect beads, made authentic by two misshapen ovals nestled near the clasp. She told me that if I wore them next to my skin, they would take away my anger.

And I have her 1938 unabridged Webster's dictionary, with an assortment of dried four-leaf clovers pressed between the pages at the letter *F*.

And I have her eternal love, which is proven by the events described in this story and by the special protection she gives to my oldest child, who leads what can only be characterized as a charmed life.

A HEART'S CALL AWAY

Mary Fuller

Mary Fuller, sixty-three, lives in Newport Beach, California. A registered nurse, in 1997 she fulfilled a lifetime dream when she got her bachelor's degree in comparative literature. Her hobbies include reading, bridge, Pilates, and spending time with her six grandchildren.

I am discovering that birds, feathers, and wings are symbolic to many of us for various reasons. They touch many levels of human experience, especially the spiritual level. What is it about birds that enables us to imagine our life as somehow filtered through the lens of their behaviors?

It is the birds' wings that speak to me. It is their phenomenal ability to free themselves from earth and roam the skies. It's no wonder that my mother came to me in the form of a large bird.

Momma died of breast cancer in 1964. I was twenty-four years old and seven months pregnant with our second son. She had just turned fifty. She did not want to worry us, so she waited to inform the family of her illness until her last year alive. This was understandable, but unfortunate.

We were heartbroken by the news. Back then, the only procedure for breast cancer was radiation or a radical mastectomy. Her small-framed body suffered through both these procedures, which seemed to me then, and even now, to be more the cause of weakening her body and of her premature death than the cancer.

My mother was from a large, warm Irish family—nine brothers and sisters, whose parents lived to a "ripe old age." When I was a child, we lived on the same street with Momma's parents, her sisters and their husbands, her brothers and their wives, and all of their children. Two of her sisters lived in Canada but brought their husbands and children to visit us for a month each summer. We were all very close.

When my grandfather and grandmother died, the family gradually moved away from each other. This was a sad happening for all of us, but especially for my mother. Gone was the noise and activity of a large family that celebrated holidays together in a loud and raucous way. Mother's world was diminished to only the noise and activity of one young daughter.

I know she missed her large family living close by, and compensated by showering all her affections on Dad and me. I was her only child. As I matured into a young woman, the relationship of mother and child blossomed into one of friendship. When she died, I not only lost my mother, but my best friend as well.

Through the years that have followed Momma's death, I have missed her terribly, especially at significant times in my life: the birth of our last four children, their baptisms, and especially their weddings and the births of their children. I feel what can only be described as a soul's deepest yearning for her. Time has allowed healing and the intellectual acceptance of the reality of her death, yet there is, and I suppose will always be, a void in my life.

It was during a particularly difficult time in my life, one of much upheaval and turmoil, that this yearning became the strongest. I needed my mother and wanted to feel her close. Not often did I—nor do I now—call out to Momma. Up to this time I had communicated with her through silent prayers from my heart, not from my voice. However, at this particular time I spoke out loud in a soft yet clear voice. I said, "I wish you were here. I need you." It is what happened after I spoke to her in this specific way that I will relate.

I had been yearning for Momma for some weeks and went to bed one night with this feeling of need in my heart. Just before awakening in the morning, I felt what could only be described as an awareness. A recognition of goodness and safety seemed to envelop me from head to toe.

It came in the form of a very large bird that encircled me with its huge wings, gathering me close and holding me fast. Instantly I felt its warmth and softness, but more so its offering of love and peace. Inside the core of my body and from the strength of old memories radiated a certain knowledge that the warmth, peace, and love surrounding me were my mother, and that she had come to me because I needed her and had called to her. I really do not know how long I was cradled in this wonderful condition. When I came to myself, all the feelings of yearning and fearfulness had evaporated. What remained was an indescribable feeling of peace.

This experience is one that I will never forget. It stands as proof to me that mothers hear and fulfill the earthly needs of those they love even though they have moved to another existence. They are more aware of our needs than we might ever suspect. The point to all this is the knowledge that we are not left alone. Each of us is only a heart's call away from access to our mother's eternal love.

ADELE

Diane deSimone

Diane deSimone, a writer, is best known as the author of *Sex and the Brain*. She has written for national magazines both here and abroad. Diane is currently working on screenplays and fiction.

She left this reality not long ago. The day before her eighty-first birthday. At three o'clock in the morning. The obituaries appeared the day of her birthday in the *New York Times* and our more local Southwest newspaper. I wrote them both. And how could I not? I loved her deeply. Her vitality, her artistry in sculpture and in life. Above all, her smile. Her wide and warm, inviting and encompassing, embracing smile.

As I was preparing for the memorial service, I looked through my photographs of her—from her youth, at the time of her marriage, with her two children, at elegant political dinners, at the piano, in her sculpture studio, in bathing suits, in satin and silk and sweaters, standing still: her soul caught for a second in a momentary frame. And there it was, in most every take, her laughter, her smile.

The phone call from the hospice had shaken me out of sleep; I had left her some seven hours before, exhausted, still needing to plan some sort of party for her birthday. As I was driving to see her body for the last time, the song that I heard her singing for my benefit was from the musical *Peter Pan*, "I'm Flying." "Look at me way up high . . ." She clearly wanted me to hear and know her exhilaration at being freed from her mortal form.

And yes, when I went into her room to visit with her body, it *was* very obvious—she *had* quickly left it. No hanging around for her. She was gone, into the ethers; ready and willing to go on to live another life. With a zing, a zest, some laughter, a smile.

But later on that day, I couldn't help but weep and plead with her to send me a message, some new message that she was all right. Perhaps things had changed for her. Perhaps her new life was not all it had been cracked up to be, after that initial sense of freedom. I needed to know. *Give me something else to hold on to,* I asked. *Please.*

Three hours later I got a phone call from my stepson, Zachary. He is nine years old. His soul is immaculate, full of laughter, too, and she had just begun to take true delight in him. He called to tell me that earlier that morning he had been awakened by a dream—and he never remembers dreams unless they are nightmares. There she was, he said, before his eyes, my mother's face and she was radiant, and smiling. She had said three words, "You are loved." Then, as quickly as she arrived, she left. She had disappeared.

THE DOVE'S MESSAGE

Lois Davis and Betty Lowe

 Lois, seventy-one, and Betty, seventy, are sisters who live together. They are both semiretired, with Lois doing part-time bookkeeping and Betty taking care of a bedridden woman a few hours each week. They enjoy gardening, quilting, and crocheting.

Our mother (with her ten-years-younger husband, who was not our father) moved to Safford, Arizona, from Albuquerque about twenty years ago to be closer to us. We weren't among her husband's favorite people, and the feeling was mutual. Therefore we drove out periodically to bring her back to town for a few days or a week at the most.

She was fine . . . a little forgetful but no Alzheimer's at eighty-four years of age. She enjoyed sitting at the windows that overlooked our patio, watching the many dozens of birds we fed each morning . . . mostly doves, some finches, cardinals, and thrushes.

Mom had, several years earlier, made arrangements when the time came for the University of Arizona to use her body in research and, when they were finished, to cremate it and give the ashes to the family, to be scattered in the foothills of the mountainous area.

She died suddenly in Safford while out hanging up clothes. Before we could get there, her husband had called the university and they had picked her up immediately.

Our younger sister arrived the following day from Los

Angeles. The three of us went out to the university to see our mother's body. She looked like she was asleep when they wheeled her out of the "cooler." The doctor in charge said he would call us when the ashes would be ready for pickup.

On the day they say our mother was cremated, a white dove came to our patio. It appeared to be exhausted and sat for hours on the same spot on an olive limb. We put grain on the table for it and it ate. We took pictures of it. It stayed around for about a week.

At no time did it ever seem to mingle with the other doves, and they acted as though it didn't exist. Then it was gone, never to be seen again.

It was the only white dove we had ever seen in the yard.

Mom knew we watched the birds a lot and would certainly notice a white dove. We feel it was a message to us that she was OK and on the other side.

MILAGRO

Pamela Hale

Pamela Hale, fifty-seven, is a writer, artist, photographer, teacher, and counselor who offers workshops on personal and organizational transformation. A licensed private pilot, she is currently working on a memoir called "Flying Lessons."

1990

No one knew whether it would be weeks or months, but she had a premonition she would die while we were gone. Why did I agree to come to Greece? Now she's in a coma and we are too far to make it home in time. They say that even if I were by her side now, she wouldn't know. But I don't believe that. She is my mother. I should be with my mother for her death.

Promotional brochures promise that Greece's glaring white sculptured buildings, set off by an electric blue sky and sea, will bleach away any spots of sadness from your soul. Yet standing on this remote beach on the isle of Tinos, all I feel is searing guilt and grief. Surely the Greek goddesses whose legends still swirl about in the waves must have some lessons for me now.

We are on a rugged, unpopulated part of this tiny island. The wind has been attacking Tinos, and last night banged on our doors and shook our windows. *Ruach*, the wind is called in Hebrew; the word also means spirit.

I turn to face the uneasy sea, ready to hear the voice behind the elements.

"I was torn, God," I tell the waves, as my second husband, Jon, walks on down the beach to explore the white marble cliffs that support it. "Of course I wanted to be with her. And yet, I wanted to take this trip with Jon, too. I didn't want to cancel our first anniversary celebration, only to have her dying process drag out over months. And I listened when Jon gently pointed out that she has manipulated me before. Perhaps she was jealous again and wanted me to miss this trip. Wanted me to choose her instead of him." I cry at my own confession.

Our family did discuss all this, a gentler voice reminds me. And Mother encouraged me to come, to embrace my new life. We decided what was important was time together. So I went to Los Angeles to take care of her for five days. She was so tiny when I was there. Couldn't have weighed over eighty pounds. It was easy for me to carry her to the toilet and back to bed. An earlier breast cancer had metastasized and was traveling through her bones and lungs. Like her mother, she wasn't going to be able to fight it off the second time.

She would periodically hold her legs in the air and cry out, obviously in pain. When I would sympathize, she would say, "It really doesn't hurt that much. I just need to whimper." Nothing was premeditated now; she was spontaneous. Old lies and pretensions had fallen away with her flesh, and now she was becoming luminous and truthful. As her body was shrinking, Spirit was growing in her. It emanated from her eyes as we asked each other the simple questions we needed to have answered.

"Are you happy?" she asked me. "Is it a good marriage?" When I nodded affirmatively and took a breath to begin elaborating, she stopped me. "That's all I need to know."

"Are you afraid, Mom?"

"No, not of death anyway. Just a little afraid of the dying."

Those words rang in my ears now. It was only yesterday that we took the boat to Mykonos, where there was a phone. While I called home, Jon waited at a small table where he could peruse the beach, so touristed compared to Tinos. I walked back from the phone booth wearing what he first mistook for a smile. It was the grimace of grief. Mom had a day left, maybe two. My brother counseled me to stay put. My daughters were with her. It was all right, my brother said.

"It seemed all right when we talked about it, but it is not all right now," I told Jon, who looked so strong and tan.

"We can go back," he offered right away. "But let's think about the reasons we decided to come. If they're still good, then we should stay. If they weren't good reasons, we should fly back, even if we might not make it in time."

Since he was able to think, we went through the reasons.

First, changing our ticket and going home now would cost a bundle. Oh, how I hoped the money wouldn't be the reason we'd stay.

Second, I had already said my good-bye. I thought about the last moments I was with her, before my friend Mary took me to the airport to fly home to Tucson. I was sitting in the den in the house I grew up in, on the old familiar cool of the green leather couch. My mother was slumped next to me, like a little girl, huddled in the nest of my arm. I stroked her hair. "My little mom," I said, making her laugh. Dad watched, and I wondered if he saw that I had always been more the mother, she more the daughter. I think we all knew that was to be our last moment together.

And third, Jon and I needed to embrace our new life together. The last two years had lifted me out of an old life too filled with darkness. I had worked hard on myself. I ought to have a Ph.D. in psychology for all the therapy I'd had. I could identify myself in victim terms: the child of a bipolar, alcoholic mother; the ex-wife of an emotionally abusive husband; the mother of two daughters trying to avoid their own versions of the family cancers. Instead I was in love with the clear light of Tucson, with my new husband's easy style, with the Great Wind that had carried me into my new chapter, and with the sensuality of Greece. I felt like Persephone had ruled much of my early life, which had been in the underworld. Now Aphrodite and Hera were luring me with the promise I could be a good and happy wife. I was trying to follow my heart.

I remembered the moment Mother surprised me by putting her seal of approval on Jon. We had been earning our trip here, piling up frequent flier miles on trips between his Tucson and my Los Angeles. We had become serious, so he came for Christmas to meet my parents and spend his first holiday with my daughters. I had Mother and Dad over for brunch, a preemptive strike against the drinking I knew she would do if we waited for the sun to set.

I bustled nervously in the kitchen while I left Jon to the interview I knew was being carried on in the living room. After fifteen minutes or so, Mother walked into the kitchen and put her hand over mine, stopping the stirring I was doing to the hollandaise sauce. I looked up to see what her face would tell me. Her eyes were clear, direct. She smiled. "Oh, Pam, he's wonderful," she said tenderly. I was surprised by my intense relief. I thought I had become so independent of her.

We ended our Mykonos visit by deciding that the quality good-bye had already taken place, and that returning early would be frustrating and futile. Next week would be soon enough to reunite with family and have the memorial service.

So here I am on the edge of this tiny cove, facing into the Aegean Sea, standing on an island made of white marble. Jon is walking down to the end of the beach, where sparkling rocks are topped by a solitary, tiny, one-room church. Like the hundreds of other family shrines on Tinos, this one must have been made by family members who brought materials from another part of the island by boat.

This whole island is a shrine of sorts, a destination visited each year by Greek religious seekers who get off the boat and crawl up the cobblestoned hill to the large church at the top of the steep main street. During the religious festival, vendors line the sidewalks to sell icons and candles as tall as spears. The church ceiling is filled with tiny hanging sculptures: parts of the body, boats, hearts, or whatever symbols fit the suffering the pilgrim is praying to have relieved. The Greek version of the Mexican *milagros* we see around Tucson.

I am a pilgrim here on this beach, asking the waves for help. I need to build a shrine inside to my dying mother, or at least to have a symbol to heal her suffering, and mine. I need a *milagro*, a miracle.

"Is she dead or alive?" I am asking Spirit, or perhaps Poseidon.

"She hovers in between," I hear the waves tell me.

"I'm so sorry I'm not with her," I confess as sobs rise up and undulate through me.

"But haven't you always believed that the connection between loved ones goes far beyond the physical and the verbal?" the saltwater seems to ask me.

"Yes, but right now I need the physical. I need a literal sign, something to tell me that she knows I am with her, that I love her." I am feeling slightly crazed now, glad that Jon is out of earshot.

The silence leaves me without anything more to say to the waves, so I turn to walk down the beach to join Jon. After my first step, I am stopped in my tracks. In front of me lies a rock shaped like a perfect heart. It is about four inches wide, three or four inches high, and its thickness varies between an inch or two. It is made of white marble. Alabaster, translucent in its thinner parts and veined in a soft gold. It fits perfectly in my hand.

2001

I study the Catalina Mountains that seem to rise up right out of the backyard of our Tucson house. A decade has passed since my mother left earth, yet the forms of rock and light and shadow look the same to me. The only difference is that they were once exotic and now they represent home. They endure passing weather and have taken on the role of the sea; they are vast, deep, changing yet constant.

I have felt my mother many times, especially lately. Now, too, I am a breast cancer survivor. Like my mother, I have had a mastectomy, and am undergoing chemotherapy. Like her, I worry sometimes that the cancer could return to my lungs or to my bones. I could be lying there holding my legs in the air and crying out, not wanting my daughter to leave me.

But I don't think that's what's ahead. I have spent a lot of energy in the last ten years sifting seeds: Which ones are common to my mother and me, and which are mine alone? What am I to heal from? Which family cancers can I release? How am I bonded to my mother and how am I totally separate from her? I did not expect to still be asking these questions at fifty-seven.

My cancers don't have to be hidden the way hers were.

Her culture attached shame to every insidious disease she suffered. My healing journey is far from the private hell she and her mother felt obliged to inhabit. I am floated along a web of prayers and caring. My prognosis is great and I plan to die late, surrounded by the family I have asked to stay with me.

I don't think of my mother every day. But often she makes her way here, across the waves. Even in the desert she appears, sometimes in someone's laugh, other times vibrating from one of her pieces of jewelry, wading through the waters of a dream, or appearing at the end of my bed to protect me. She is asking me to sort us out, to give her back what is hers, to take what is mine and to live it out. She is, for me now, an ally. I am learning to take her gifts and to learn from her tragedies and release them.

I go out into the desert to walk. I am making my way through the bed of an ancient sea. I can see its influence in the wavy shapes of cactus and in the pearly light that reminds me of Tinos. Wherever I look, there are creations. Rocks here have lives of their own, where lizards and rabbits and quail try to survive and leave their legacies. Often I spot a rock shaped like a heart, and like to regard it as a sign that once again love has washed up right under my feet.

I return to my office, where I keep an altar and meditation cushion by the window, where birds feed just through the glass. Among my sacred objects on the sill is the Greek alabaster heart. It is cold, until I warm it in my hands. It needs me as much as I need it. Love needs to be held right in my hands, transformed from stone to flesh, brought to life again each day. I know in this moment that whether I live one more day or forty more years, it is love that is healing me.

My mother has passed me that gift.

THE FRAGRANCE OF ROSES

Kathy Locarano

A retired health care worker, Kathy Locarano grew up in a Hispanic community in the Southwest. Bilingual, she contributed to the book *Corazon Contento: Sonoran Recipes and Stories from the Heart.*

I was the "change of life" baby, the last one to be born in a family of nine brothers and sisters. When I came along, my mom and dad had mellowed out, and they were ready to enjoy me.

My mother and I became very close over the years. She shared all her dreams with me, and also some of the bad times. I could talk to her about anything. She often gave me advice about life and was never too busy to listen to me.

Mom's favorite flower was the rose and she wore rose water and glycerin as a fragrance. When Mom hugged and kissed me, I always smelled the roses.

I respected my mom a lot. She was liberated enough to talk about any subject and allowed me to express myself. In those days, in the Hispanic culture, women were not allowed to express their opinions.

When I was old enough to go out with my friends, it was usually to the local dance. My mom would wait up for me. She was eager to hear how my evening went and didn't want to hear that I was a wallflower. She wanted to know how many times I danced and whether the young men were handsome.

As we sat there on the bed and I relived my evening to

my mom, her eyes would sparkle as she recalled her own memories from long ago. A faint smile would appear on her lips, as if she were being transformed into a young girl again. Sometimes I would add a little bit to my stories, just to see Mom's expression.

I would say, "Mom, you should have seen James. He was tall with green eyes and black hair. All the girls were jealous of me."

After I finished telling about my experiences, Mom would hug and kiss me good night. I felt so lucky that I had a mother who cared and who loved me so much. I'll never forget those days.

Now that my mom is gone, I miss those times. I don't have a daughter to relive my youth with. But when I have a quiet moment, I can smell the roses, and I know my mom is there with me. Now the fragrance of roses is with me, whether I'm sad or happy. She always sends her love through the fragrance of roses.

A VISIT FROM SARAH'S GREAT-GRANDMOTHER

Fran Haggerty

Originally from Cleveland, Ohio, Fran Haggerty, fifty-eight, is a mental health family therapist. She is currently working with the juvenile court system in a diversion program. In her spare time she hikes, works out, and is a mounted volunteer with the National Park System.

My mother and I were really close when I was growing up. She was a stay-at-home mother and her first priority was her family, for she loved her husband and her children more than anything.

After I moved west we remained close, but it was a long-distance relationship. In our family we always felt that the way to have an extra special experience was to share it, so we shared by talking on the phone all the time.

When my mother died before her first great-grandchild arrived, it seemed like I missed her more than ever. When Sarah was born, I thought about my mother a whole lot. For the first time, I really understood how my mother felt when her first grandchild was born. It was like, "Yeah, I finally get it now." Of course, I knew what it was to love your kids because they are the center of your life, but it's just a different thing with your grandchildren.

I was really pissed that my mother was gone and I couldn't share this baby with her, because I knew it would make the experience even more wonderful—this really great experience would have been even grander if she were here.

One day the baby was fussy and I was sitting there rocking her in an old antique rocking chair. It was twilight and I was humming softly and really trying to quiet myself so the baby would also quiet. Thinking back on it, I was probably in a meditative state as I rocked. Suddenly this overwhelming love washed over me and I became my mother. She was there, through me, helping me quiet the baby down and love her and soothe her and tell her that she's the most wonderful thing in the world.

Almost immediately Sarah relaxed. She settled and quieted, putting her head on my shoulder as she finally gave in to sleep.

After that there were three or more times with Sarah where this same feeling washed over me, where I was my mother. It always came when I was not expecting it, and I always knew it was an extraordinary gift.

It was a wonderful experience to connect with my mother through this special baby, her great-grandchild.

THE OPERA NOTE

Dixie Nelson

Dixie Nelson, forty one, lives in Denver, Colorado, with her husband and four daughters. She is a Reiki master/practitioner and is interested in all aspects of energy healing. Dixie owns a small business where she manufactures and sells specialty key chains.

My mother died just short of her fifty-fourth birthday, in July of 1980. I was twenty at the time, just beginning to tap into the wounds of my troubled relationship with my mother, and on the threshold of what would be nearly twenty years of intense personal discovery and healing.

An active alcoholic, my mother was a soul in search of love. She had been very pained by her own choices in life, and also by those of my father, who divorced her many years earlier when I was a small child.

When I was twelve, I had to choose which parent I would live with. After trying it out with my mother, it became obvious to those around me that it would be best for me to live with my father. Although my choice didn't rest well in my mother's heart, it was eventually accepted and our time together was more appreciated, since it was by desire rather than through obligation.

It was during this time together—in what I would call pre-reconciliation—that my mom was diagnosed with breast cancer. Her battle was fast and furious. Thankfully, her passing was a true blessing for her spirit to be free at last.

I was fortunate to have the opportunity to nurture my mother, who wasn't able to fully nurture herself or her children in life, and help her find some joy and unconditional love the last months of her stay on earth.

Each year, on the anniversary of her death, on her birthday, and especially on Mother's Day, I would find a way to honor her and show my respect, in prayer, in tears, or in silence.

Upon the birth of each of my three daughters, I felt her absence (looking back now, perhaps it was her presence!). I knew that no matter what her mothering skills had been in my childhood, she would have been the best grandmother in the world.

Last year on Mother's Day, I felt a strong desire to pay homage in a way that would bring about spiritual peace. Two months earlier I had met an incredible man, and in a short period of time we had fallen in love. He would be witness to the ceremony, which I will soon describe.

My mother had been an aspiring opera singer. I had heard from people who knew her in her singing days that her voice was a glorious artistic gift. Even my father, who rarely spoke a kind word of her, praised the voice she was given.

My father sold his house, and during the process of moving had come across reel-to-reel tapes of my mother singing an opera piece. He sent them to me. It took me several years to turn these tapes into cassettes so I too could share the beauty of my mother's talent. I knew the time to listen had to be chosen thoughtfully—obviously it would be on Mother's Day.

I created a shrine for the occasion, with candles, beautiful photos of my mom when she was younger, her college yearbooks, and a most sacred charm from a necklace that she had been wearing as she left her body. I wore her first wedding band, which I've always cherished and have worn at different times since her death, and I donned a blouse that been hers in the 1940s and that I had never worn. With the mood set, my sweetheart and I held hands, had a moment of meditation, and began the tape.

My mother's enchanting voice filled our sacred space with melodious echoings and angelic presence. In the precise moment in which her voice reached its climactic pitch, a candlestick exploded with a fury of shattered crystal and spilled wax. The chills surged through our bodies in evidence of the eccentricity of the occurrence, yet we were stilled by the serenity of the presence. The presence of my mother. I knew then what I had always hoped—that my mother was singing with the angels, where she belonged.

Her gift to me on that day will always be a reminder that a mother's love is eternal. I am forever grateful.

I love you, Mommy!

THE GOOD-BYE ANGEL

Linda Blanchard

Linda Blanchard, fifty-three, worked for the telephone company for fifteen years in Illinois, Oklahoma, and Colorado. She has also done public relations work in Elko, Nevada, where she now lives. In her spare time Linda enjoys playing golf and bridge.

As long as we lived away from each other, my mother and I got along great. But at home together, we didn't do as well. I don't think she loved me as much as she did the other kids. Because of those feelings, I rebelled against her, even as an adult. Now that I'm a mother, I realize that I probably hurt her a lot more than I knew.

After her heart attack I immediately made airline reservations to go visit her. Then, after everyone assured me that she was doing fine, I decided to wait until she was released from the hospital so that I could take care of her at home.

I had a ticket to go on Saturday and she had another heart attack that Friday night.

That night I was in bed when I had this dream or vision or whatever. My mother appeared before me as an angel. I could see her and she had long, flowing auburn hair and was wearing a robe that almost looked like a choir robe. Looking like a lot younger version of herself, she reminded me a lot of me when I saw her.

She was floating above my head when she spoke.

"All is forgiven," she said. "There is joy."

And then she disappeared.

I fell back asleep. I don't know how long it was after my vision that the phone rang and I was told that my mother had died.

THE LOVE CONNECTION

Linda Lewis

Linda Lewis and her husband own a woodworking shop where she worked for twenty-five years. She likes to work with people and in her spare time she helps her Rotary Club with fund-raising and clothing drives. Linda, fifty-nine, and the mother of four children, also does volunteer work with the Sisters of Saint Joseph of Carondolet.

I experienced unconditional love from my mother. She was completely loyal, never took sides or judged, and was always very supportive. She also had an uncanny sense of knowing when I needed to talk to her. When I needed her, she'd call. My mother really was my best friend.

It wasn't always that way. Before my parents met, my mother was a governess for the Kennedy family. Her charges included Ted, who was a little boy then, Rosemary, and their sisters. This was during the time that Joseph Kennedy was the U.S. ambassador to England. She left that job to marry my father.

When I was growing up, I always felt like my mother was expecting us to be perfect, like the Kennedy children. Of course, that wasn't it at all and I wasted a lot of good years resenting her. Even after I grew up, I was angry and felt like she was still trying to control me. I kind of made my mother-in-law my mother, yet even then my own mother never said anything. Years later when I apologized for my behavior, Momma was gracious and loving and always said, "There's nothing to apologize for."

My mother was a diabetic and she had open-heart surgery twice in a ten-day period. The doctors gave her a 2 percent chance of pulling through, yet she did and then went on to live another three years. It was as though she knew that we had things to resolve, and those three years were our open, loving, and caring times.

We belonged to the same sorority, Alpha Omicron Pi, and about a month before she died, my mother and I went to a sorority luncheon at the Hotel Del Coronado on Coronado Island. As we were walking out, she turned to me and said, "I want you to know that if anything happens to me, I'm ready to go."

My mother got peritonitis, an inflammation of the membrane that lines the abdomen, and after her surgery, the doctors didn't sew her up because they needed to go in the next day to make sure that they had removed all of the dead tissue.

While she came out of surgery, she never came out of the anesthetic. Painted with betadine, her body blew up like the balloon ladies you see in circuses, and she lapsed into a coma. Although she could barely move, my sister and I would talk to her. I knew she heard us because I could feel the slightest pressure coming from her hands.

She died in a California hospital. When I called my son to tell him, I was startled when he asked if she died at five-thirty that morning.

"Yes," I said.

"I thought so," he replied, "because I was awakened at that time by her presence."

Let me digress here to say that although I've always leaned toward believing in these kinds of spiritual events, I never talked about them. It was only after my children, who are very sensitive to metaphysical things, started sharing their experiences that I began to open up. Before that, I never told anyone because I didn't want others to think I was crazy.

Because my mother had told me she was ready to leave, it made it easier for me to let go, to not fight her death. But it still wasn't easy.

After my mother died, we were home making arrangements for her services, and it just got to be too much for me. I went wailing into my bedroom and suddenly I smelled her betadine. Instantly I knew that it was my mother telling me to calm down and that she was OK.

Two weeks later I was driving home from California. I was anxious about the trip and still grieving. Going into Yuma, which is on the Arizona-California border, I reached for something in the car and suddenly smelled the betadine again and knew she was with me.

Then a year after her death I was in my living room. It was dark out and I hadn't turned the lights on yet. No one was home, and as I sat in the middle of the couch I was feeling terribly lost and forlorn. A totally helpless feeling came over me, and I didn't know what to do. Suddenly I felt this wisp of a hug. It was as though someone had given me a brief hug and pulled their arms away fast. I felt it above both of my elbows on my arms, and I knew it was my mother telling me that everything was OK.

Over the years, I've learned that not everyone is fortunate enough to recognize these kinds of connections. I'm sure I probably had visitations from my grandmother and, for whatever reason, was not receptive to receiving them. My sister has also probably had Mom visit her and was unaware of it.

Just because one child receives something from her

mother and another doesn't, does not mean that the
mother loved one more than the other. It just means that
for whatever reason, the connection is coming to that
child. It helps to be open.

ANGELS OF LOVE AND FORGIVENESS

Anonymous

My life began in April of 1955, when I was born into a dysfunctional and abusive family. I am the middle of five children and the first of two girls. We were all abused in many different ways: physically, mentally, and emotionally. I was left with feelings and thoughts of anger, spite, self-doubt, unworthiness, and shame.

I have always loved people and felt that others were more important than I was. Over time, I developed a pattern of codependency that followed me through life.

My mother, who had also been severely abused, was psychologically classified as being just below a manic-depressive level. As a child I could not understand her extreme mood swings that ranged from laughter and excitement one minute to anger and sadness the next. Yelling, screaming, and crying were an everyday experience in our home.

My father was a doctor who worked very hard and kept long hours. One day, when I was twelve years old, he finally decided that he could not handle my mother's condition anymore, and he left us.

Later in my life, while going to college to become a social worker, I attended several classes that discussed the human psyche. Finally I was able to better understand my mother's problems.

Although I recognized certain family patterns, I still

found it difficult to make the necessary changes to bring about love and peace in my own life.

I have had two near-death experiences. The last one happened during the birth of my last child. This experience had a profound effect on me and left me with a desire to heal and change my life. I wanted to have a life filled with love, peace, and harmony.

As time went on, my mother's condition grew worse. Every conversation I had with her ended in a heated argument. In 1993, I came to realize that when we finished our conversations, I would, in turn, take out my frustrations on my own children. I decided that this was not what I wanted for my family.

At the time, I did not have the strength to deal with my mother, so I chose not to speak with her anymore. I made this decision with a clear mind and heart, not because I didn't love my mother, but so I could begin to have a healthier and happier relationship with my own family.

A few years later, just prior to my mother's death, I started a career as a spiritual counselor. Through my meditations I began to understand that I was to teach people, using the powerful cures of love and forgiveness, to help them heal themselves. Using myself as an example, I often explained how I had dealt with my own abusive experiences.

During a meditation, on the Sunday just prior to her death, my mother's spirit appeared. And then I heard, "Heal thy mother; for in healing thy mother, thou will heal thyself."

I mentally placed my hands on my mother's head, and a brilliant green light filled her body. The angels then asked me to walk her into this bright light that had appeared. At this point in my life, I still had a lot of anger toward my mother, and I would not do what they asked.

The following Wednesday, while counseling someone

whose mother was manic-depressive, I heard the angels say, "You can use your mother and how you dealt with your situation as an example, but do not speak of her in an ill way anymore." Intuitively I knew at this point that she would soon die. I was right, for a few days later I learned that she had died that same day.

At the time of her death, my mother lived in Michigan, and I had not talked to her in over two years. When I went to identify her body, I experienced all the pain she had felt, and caused, during her lifetime. I knelt down to pray for her, and although I was alone in an empty room, there was a sudden loud bang. It was then that my mother's spirit came to me and said, "Do not pray for me, I am fine."

I had felt guilty for not walking her into the angelic light, so I asked to be taken back to that time. I saw my mother's spirit, but this time Jesus was standing next to her. I mentally placed my hands on her, and suddenly her body dropped to the ground like a piece of cloth. Underneath her was a blinding gold light, which I saw as the ultimate light of Spirit.

I was told that she had been my disciplinarian and that she had taught me many powerful lessons in this life. I knew then that she had been one of my teachers. Relief washed over me, along with the sudden realization that she had helped me to release a lot of my karma.

When I returned from Michigan, a friend gave me a plant in memory of my mother. At that point, the angels told me that my mother had sent it to me in an indirect way, through my friend, with her love. This was quite a shock to me because it was in sharp contrast to how my mother had been in life.

A short time later, my sister sent me a box of pictures of my mother. When I first opened the box, I felt a great deal of pain. But within a moment my mother's spirit appeared, this time as a golden angel.

She told me that she had always loved me and that these memories were her gift to me. I felt an overwhelming love emanating from her, which soon dissolved my pain. When she came to me as this angel, healed of her pain, I knew she was with me to help heal mine.

My mother's spirit stayed with me constantly until the fall of 1996, when I was to appear in court against my ex-husband. While my mother had had two divorces in her life, she had never had the strength to stand up for herself or to fight back in court.

After I succeeded in having the case dismissed, I went back to work. My mother appeared again and said, "You have accomplished what I could not. I am done working with you; it's time to help the other kids."

I understood then that she had come back to help our family heal.

Her passing has begun the healing of many generations of pain and abuse for our entire family. Since she has passed on, I have seen my brothers and sister regain their self-esteem and self-confidence. All of our lives have been changing for the better.

For instance, my brother, who had never felt worthy of a promotion, received one within six months of my mother's death. He is finally beginning to feel more confident and proud of himself.

My sister is trying to reunite our family, and we have all begun to communicate and share with each other as a result of her efforts.

Every time I think of my mother, I feel her guiding me and helping me to heal. I have become more independent and there are often times, during difficult situations, when I see my mother's hands at work helping all of us.

Recently I have begun to understand that during my

first near-death experience, when I stood over my still body, I made the choice to stay and finish the karma that had to be dealt with. I feel that even though I may not have liked those lessons, I have learned well from them. Through them my self-esteem and my self-worth have been restored. I have learned to unconditionally love others and myself, and to forgive others as I forgive myself.

My mother has also been with me during this writing. She is guiding me in how best to tell this story in a way that it may help others. She smiles quietly and chuckles about how such a blessing can come out of a past that is perceived to be so horrible.

She reminds us all to love, forgive, and heal the past. For it is only through love and forgiveness that we are able to heal.

ROSIE

Wendy Sizer

Wendy Sizer, fifty-three, works as a freelance
writer. Her mother, Barbara Loudon Sizer Rogers,
taught her by example to take courage, have
courage, and encourage. For that Wendy remains
forever grateful.

When Mom took Rosie into her life, Rosie was already
a full-grown cat. No one really knew how old she was, but
she was no kitten. She was part Burmese, part Heinz 57.

After several years, Mom, a widow for sixteen years, remarried and moved to Prouts Neck, Maine, a small penin-
sula near Portland where Winslow Homer once had his
studio.

Mom married a man with a big standard poodle by the
name of Marc. One day Marc nearly killed Rosie when he
cornered her in an upstairs bathroom. Rosie had been de-
clawed, so her defenses were minimal.

After that incident, Rosie stayed upstairs in Mom's
room. The door to the room had a hook-and-eye latch that
permitted the door to stay open just enough for Rosie to
go in and out if she wanted, but not let Marc in. Rosie
would venture downstairs on occasion, but only if Marc
was outside and if few people were around. The living
room was usually filled with people coming and going, so
these occasions were rare.

Mom and Rosie were devoted to one another. The marriage wasn't all that great, so Mom looked to Rosie often
for solace and company. Rosie slept with Mom every

night, wrapped around her neck or cuddled up somewhere close.

In 1992, when mom died at eighty-one of an abdominal aneurysm, Rosie was bereft. Mom was in the hospital, so the night she died, I slept in Mom's bed at her home so I could be there for and with Rosie.

A few days later we had a memorial service for Mom at the house. Mom wasn't much of a churchgoer, and we figured she'd want a service close to the ocean that she loved and the garden that she designed and built. About thirty or forty people came to this little service, held in the living room. We all formed a circle, and people volunteered their stories about their times with Mom.

The overflow of people went up the stairs. I'd say probably eight to ten people sat on the stairs, not quite all the way to the top.

Lo and behold, in the middle of the service, Rosie came out of Mom's room near the top of the stairs, looked out between the banister railings, and then began to walk down the stairs weaving her way between people sitting there.

She arrived at the bottom step, walked to the inside of the circle we had formed, looked around, and then walked back upstairs again.

Those people who didn't know Rosie thought it was cute.

Those of us who knew how shy she was, namely my sister, my niece, and I, all looked at each other knowing Mom had just given us a sign that she was A-OK.

THE STORY OF RUTH

Ruth Cousins Hobbs

Ruth Cousins Hobbs is carrying on the family business that was her parents' before their deaths. She is fifty-nine and lives in Gallup, New Mexico.

My mother, Jean Cousins, was a very special woman. She went to Arizona in 1925 with her single mother, and later with my father, Bill, forged a fascinating life. They were Indian traders for many years at the Wide Ruins Trading Post at Kin Teel, Arizona, where my brother, Edward, and I were raised among the hustle and bustle of an old-time trading post. The book *Tales from Wide Ruins* recounts the story of my parents' lives together. The editor for that book, Mary Tate Engels, described my mother in this way: "She was the most optimistic, upbeat person I have ever met. She'd greet each day by looking out the window and saying 'I wonder what good things will happen to us today.'"

In 1993, fifty-nine years after marrying my father, my mother died of emphysema.

When I lost my mother, I lost my very best friend, my champion, my confidante. Then when little things started happening, I was comforted and started feeling not quite alone. I knew that my mother was near me.

One of the most striking things occurred at a time when I had a lot of problems going on in my life. I was concerned about my dad, who was well into his eighties and grieving for his wife, and I was also worried about my business, which I had bought from my mother, who had started it.

I'm always trying to get organized and straightened out, and one day I went home to sort through my mother's papers. When I opened a box that I had been through many times before, the first thing I saw was a note in my mother's handwriting that read, "Fear not. I am with you and I will uphold you with my victorious right hand."

I had never seen it before. To me, that was the most uncanny sense of her speaking to me from beyond, because of what was going on in my life at the time. She knew I needed her.

Oftentimes something will happen, and I'll sit and cry with that letter, and I'll say, "I need you to hold me a little longer." I always feel immensely better.

I've made a cookbook. I've typed the recipes we've used over the years and pasted family pictures in it. It won't mean anything to anyone but me and maybe my kids. I took the note and pasted it in the cookbook. But first I made a copy and stuck it on the refrigerator.

When *Tales from Wide Ruins* was published after my mother's death, I knew how pleased she was. I felt like she was guiding me to get Dad to tell his stories so that a book could be put together. My father wouldn't do it on his own; Mother had a hand in it. This book would never have been completed if she had not been pushing from somewhere. There are times when the sense of her being here is unbelievable.

My mother loved Fig Newtons and we always had them in the store to go with our morning coffee. One day I came in and the two Navajo girls who worked for me, who knew my mother and called her Grandma, said, "Grandma was here this morning."

When I asked why they thought so, they told me to go look at the package of cookies in the back of the store.

The box had come with Fig Newtons packaged in four cellophane sleeves. Inside one of the unbroken packages there were three cookies missing.

"Grandma likes Fig Newtons. She was here," one of the girls said, never doubting for a moment that my mother had come calling.

Another time, they were putting up Christmas decorations in the store and the ornaments on top of one of the displays kept falling down. "Grandma doesn't like them there," they said. When they moved the ornaments, there was no problem. They feel a sense of her being here periodically.

The little things continue to happen, assuring me that I am never quite alone.

MOTHER'S DAY

Maureen Jones-Ryan, Ph.D.

Dr. Maureen Jones-Ryan, a psychotherapist, is the executive director of the Sexual Assault Recovery Institute in Phoenix, Arizona. A third-generation feminist, she has recently written *Sorology: The Study of Friendships Between and Among Womyn*. Maureen, fifty-seven, lives in Carefree, Arizona.

Both my grandmother, Nana, and my mother were feminists before the term was familiar. Both were born and raised in the same small New England town in which I was born and raised: Auburn, Massachusetts. Both were womyn other mothers turned to for advice regarding birth control, child rearing, and for teaching their own children about menstruation and conception.

Nana, in fact, had monthly meetings in her parlor on Sunday afternoons to instruct womyn in the prevention of pregnancies. She was quite controversial in the town and was warned repeatedly by the local police to cease and desist.

She persisted in her "educational Sunday get-togethers" until one Sunday three men from the town broke into the gathering and roughed up my grandmother and several womyn. My mother was only eight at the time and she recalled the terror mixed with the pride she felt in her mother's courage.

Mother carried on Nana's work, and I, in turn, carried on Mother's work.

Nana was ninety-two when she passed on Mother's

Day in 1953. I was a young girl of eight and did not know that my first introduction to this part of life would be repeated the next year, when my father died at forty-nine.

Nana and Daddy had not spoken to each other for years. No one could remember what caused the original rift, but even us kids were painfully aware of the great sadness the estrangement between her mother and our father, Harold, brought our mother.

Prior to the disaffection between Nana and Daddy, they had enjoyed playing music together at family gatherings. Daddy played the violin and Nana the piano. Somewhere in the dispute between the two, Nana sold Daddy's beloved violin. He never saw it again; supporting Mother and us four girls, he was never able to afford to replace it.

Shortly after Daddy's death, and a year after the death of Nana, Mother won the derisive laughter of her sisters and the curious awe of us children when she told us that she had received a message from Nana assuring her that not only was the rift between her and Harold closed but that they had become fast friends and were again enjoying playing music together.

For months, Mother endured the ribbing and teasing of the family regarding her "message" from Nana. On Mother's Day of that year, 1954, Mother awoke to find Daddy's violin beside her on the bed she had shared with him for over twenty-five years.

Skeptics in the family proposed a variety of plausible explanations for how it came to be returned on the anniversary of Nana's death. But I knew Mother had received a tangible gift from Nana.

A few years prior to her death, my mother gifted me with Daddy's violin. Although other members of the family wanted it, she expressed to my sisters and me that I was the fortunate recipient as I was blessed with the ability to accept the truth of its history. It remains in the family, as I gave it to my son Bobby.

The story, however, does not end there. On Mother's Day, May 10, 1992, my beloved mother died. Although it was a different date from the Mother's Day passing of Nana, it was the same holiday.

Mother had lost her hearing to scarlet fever when she was six years old. Throughout my childhood I served as Mother's hearing assistant in groups. She did not speak American Sign but read lips expeditiously. I would sit at her feet and by gently touching her left leg or right leg I would indicate the direction she should look to follow the conversation.

Since shortly after Mother's death I have been gifted by her gentle touch on my legs. She touches me when I most need her direction: right leg for "yes" and left leg for "no." Should I undergo the recommended surgery?—right leg. Should I pursue the lawsuit against my former colleague?—left leg. It is only the most perplexing questions she seems to intercede on, and then only after I have suffered the angst of wrestling with the question for some length of time.

My daughter Margaret (named after both Nana and Mother) is now an attorney in Turkey carrying on the family tradition of working with womyn less privileged than we.

She is aware of Mother's communications with me. It is important to me that she is open to the possibility that I, too, after death, will communicate with her and that, in turn, she will be able to communicate with her daughter, my granddaughter, Aleksandriya.

JUNGLE VEIL

Mary Schaefer

Artist Mary Schaefer's oil paintings are found in corporate and private collections throughout the world. Much of her desire to paint came from years of adventurous travel to remote parts of the planet with her husband, Art, a mining engineer. The love of the Southwest and exposure to the diversity of people's cultures have been her greatest inspiration.

My mother spent my lifetime protecting me. In many ways, that followed me throughout my life, even after she was gone. She always worried that something would happen to me or that I might become a fallen woman. Mother probably intuitively knew that I tried to keep much of the truth from her.

My husband, Art, is a mining engineer and his work took us to many primitive, remote parts of the world. We weren't always safe. For instance, we landed in Managua, Nicaragua, in 1978, on the day the revolution had begun between the Sandinistas and Somoza, who was then president. As we deplaned we learned that the Sandinistas had destroyed our hotel with machine-gun fire. Things went downhill from there, since America was at that time Somoza's ally.

We were the enemy, and we knew that the jungle did not offer us safe haven. But for the moment, we felt it could hide us. The mines and mining camp that Art was to inspect were in the middle of nests of Sandinistas. This was their hideout territory, on the eastern side of their country, close to the Caribbean. Since returning to the States was not an option, we had no choice but to go forward.

We tried to believe that our annual trip deep into the jungle would be safe for the next two weeks, as it had always been in the past. Nothing but beauty had ever surrounded us. The scents of the jungle were unique and special. There was a sweetness and a dewiness that always permeated the air and filled me with a sense of peace and tranquility.

Our two weeks were uneventful, thank God.

Then, the day before we were to leave, one of my husband's friends was assassinated. On our way to Managua our plane crash-landed in Siuna, a tiny jungle community in the center of the Sandinistas' stronghold. There was no police department. A legal system was unheard of. The only equalizers the natives had against intruders were their machetes. And we didn't even have those.

Luckily someone realized that we were in great danger and led us to a little shack where there was a man who spoke broken English. He had our lifeline, a ham radio. Somehow we got word out to my mother that we would be delayed, without any explanation of why. Of course, every newspaper in the United States carried the story in bold letters on their front pages that revolution had broken out in Nicaragua. But at least she'd know that we were still alive.

We needed a safe, well-hidden place to sleep and hide from the revolutionaries. A total stranger, a Canadian, whisked us into the hills to a deserted mining house and provided us with armed guards that walked the periphery of our little house all night long.

The next day we flew to Managua, where conditions had gotten worse and Americans were in grave danger.

After a harrowing night we arrived at the airport and were finally on our way home.

And all during this adventure I felt my mother's presence while she followed me relentlessly around the world, keeping me under her wing.

Which is not to say that I shared all of the details of that particular trip with her. I had always been an obedient daughter, but I rarely shared my stories with my mother for fear that the worrying would be too much for her.

Now we were back in Tucson with only memories of our past dangers and safe, I thought. No guards, no guns or machetes, just peace and safety. But I was to find out that our dangers were of a different breed, but no less perilous and just as lethal. And me still without a machete.

My dear mother, friend, and protector was stricken with cancer and left me. My shield against evil that I as a youth had resented so often was gone. Neither one of us was ready to let go. Proof that she spreads her wings of safety about me even now is in a little incident that occurred a few months after I lost her in 1993.

I was returning to my car at a fancy shopping mall when I saw two people standing beside their car, which was near mine. They had been waiting for me. This was during a rash of car-jackings, and some people had recently been murdered for their cars.

The two people yelled to me to come; they had something to show me. They were insistent beyond reason, which is what alerted me.

With their continued urgings, I became frightened. Where was that protective veil I so often had and needed now?

I fumbled the keys, my packages, everything, while trying to reach my car door quickly and unlock it. At that moment I screamed at the people to leave me alone and to go away!

To my shock and amazement, the voice that emerged from my lips was not my own. It was a booming, threatening voice with a Spanish accent. I recognized it as my mother's immediately. Mother was always capable of drawing great respect by the absoluteness of her commands. No one questioned her authority, for she left nothing to the imagination.

It was here, in this shopping mall parking lot, that she gave me my first and only overt sign that she was still with me. Suddenly there was a sweetness and a dewiness in the air, filling me with a sense of peace and tranquility. I was safe again as the scent of the jungle reappeared. I knew this meant that she had always been there when I needed her.

Not even in death had she lost the power of her shield to protect me.

She watches over me every day in my painting studio, which was the place she most loved to be with me. Every now and then I feel her presence, so I turn to look at her photograph that looks directly at me at my easel, and she smiles at me. I catch her approving smile filled with contented gentleness. Thank goodness she has finally earned her peace and knows that I am now captured in a web of safety I've woven on my own. She has only one place to watch over me, in my studio where I feel her most.

Her angel arms continue to spread a protective veil over my life, and now we smell the scent of the jungle together in peace.

FOOTPRINTS

Janet M. Labrecque

Janet Labrecque, fifty-nine, is a published poet whose interests include photography, midwestern and eastern box turtles, and desert tortoises.

My mom was confined to a wheelchair for a number of years after losing both legs to complications from diabetes. Undeterred by this and related ailments, her spirits remained high as she continued her usual activities, which included weekly visits to speak to new amputees at the rehab center ("If I can do it at eighty-five, so can you!").

The 250-mile distance between us made frequent visits difficult, but I always managed a trip when a crisis arose. After one particularly serious surgery, she claimed to have been visited by her deceased mother and sister, as well as by a young woman she had not recognized who had brought along a two-year-old boy.

Sure that my mother had been hallucinating, my sister glanced at the patient in the next bed, who promptly remarked, "Oh, yes, your mother has truly had so many wonderful visitors today . . . especially the little boy named Christopher. He was so well-behaved, playing quietly under her bed the whole time."

My sister's skepticism quickly turned to shock and disbelief; her firstborn son, Christopher, had died at the age of two about twenty years earlier.

My mother recovered completely except for any memory of this incident.

June of 1996 was her last visit with us in New Jersey.

We spent a lovely afternoon in the backyard, where she maneuvered her wheelchair close to the goldfish pond and watched a long time, enthralled by the activities of fish and frogs, and especially enjoying the antics of the orphaned duckling I was caring for. It was a day that would prove to be the most memorable.

The following February, after a series of TIAs (ministrokes), my mother experienced a severe episode that required hospitalization. She took a turn for the worse during the night, and by midmorning had become nearly comatose.

Family members rushed to the hospital only to learn that she had passed away a half hour earlier. A nurse was standing by the bed, waiting to speak to them. She said that shortly before the end, my mother had awakened with a rosy glow about her face; she had smiled brightly as she told the nurse, "My husband will be here for me soon."

And so, my mom died rather suddenly.

Sad that I had not been with her, I tried to tell her so as I drifted off to sleep that night.

The next morning, while packing for the drive to Massachusetts for her funeral, I happened to glance out the kitchen window at our goldfish pond. It was frozen over, and the light dusting of snow we'd had during the night appeared disturbed.

Something told me to step out and have a closer look. It was then that I saw the unmistakable trail of footprints that led from the edge of the pond to its center, swirled a bit, and then stopped abruptly, going neither to the other side nor returning to the shore where they had originated.

I somehow knew my mother had stopped by for a final visit. It was to be the first of several others, none of which have been quite as tangible or graphic, but all still very real to me.

Footprints

The pond by wintry gusts worn smooth and swept of
    snow and leaves,
A gloss of blackness sank by drift of torn and lifting
    frost heaves;
Windows dark and dreaming, Polaris overhead,
A moonstone gleaming mid the stark of empty flower
    beds . . .
'Twas there that stole, through moss and fern, one
    February night,
Footprints of a soul returned, concealed 'til morning's
    light—
Tracks of snowdust gone across while earth slept
    unaware,
From banks still traced of yester-June, where once
    she'd wheeled her chair.

Beside the water's aquatint, together 'neath the trees,
A photograph of sky-blue pink and attic memories;
With bread crusts for the duckling, on her lap the cat
    a-sprawl,
Fed goldfish flashes caught by glints of sun and
    splashing waterfall.
Abiding eyes of misty gray, wistful of the years,
A twinkling moment of reprise, capricious laughter,
    seas of tears . . .
With wrinkled hands she softly brushed the breezes
    through her hair,
Bestrewn with wafting fishflakes sprinkled high into
    the air.

The fish now doze in waters chill, below the frozen
    glair,
Vermilion fadings stept upon, embossed with crystal air;

The duckling to a mallard grown and gone, the cat
    bed-spread;
The trickle of the waterfall become a silent thread.
My lady fair, beside her shining knight now sits,
    reborn:
Her sweet and gentle voice forever hushed this early
    morn—
Yet in my heart I know 'twas she, on angel feet,
    danced there,
As blooms a crocus in the place where was her chair.

THEN AND NOW

Jeanne Brownlee

Jeanne Brownlee is an art teacher in an inner-city public school. Currently working on her goal to build an equine portrait business, she is also a certified Parelli Natural Horsemanship Instructor. Jeanne lives with her family in Lexington, Kentucky.

In 1989 my son, Gary, was beginning school. Since he was not the kind of child that dealt with change well, this was a traumatic time. The thought of spending all day in kindergarten definitely held no appeal for my son, which made me very apprehensive.

The first day of school was met with trepidation by both of us.

Until Gary met Janice, his kindergarten teacher.

She was incredible—the most loving, touching, feeling person I could have hoped for. Instantly she made everything all right for my son. What could have been a traumatic experience for us was made right by this woman who was full of love.

The pleasant days of kindergarten droned on with no adverse effects. The child who had been so apprehensive about leaving home became an eager student.

Sometime later Janice's home burned to the ground. Only her family and pets were spared.

She was devastated and I really felt her grief. My family and home are very important to me, and so I knew just how important they were to Janice.

I'm not a publicly religious person, but at that time I happened to be in church one Sunday. And I asked, "What can I possibly do to help this woman get over her grief?"

Suddenly I heard a voice say to me, "Give her one of your paintings."

At first I argued with the idea. It just didn't seem right to give Janice one of my paintings. But then the voice said, "Yes. You have a God-given gift to share."

Most of my paintings were at a gallery, but I did have a few hanging on the walls at home. I walked through the house, considering each piece. Finally something drew me to one particular painting.

It was as though the large, thirty-by-forty-inch still life said, "This is me."

I'd painted it to represent the passage of life and had used roses from my garden. There was an unopened rosebud, a rose in full bloom, and a faded rose with petals that had fallen on an antique lace cloth draping a table. A rocking chair outside could be seen through a window.

The vase the roses were in belonged to a friend who had told me to go through her house to see if I wanted to borrow something to use in my paintings. I'd picked an antique opalescent vase with hand-painted roses on it. When I was finished with the painting, I titled it "Then and Now."

A surprise party for Janice was planned at the school. Friends toted gifts to replace the many things she had lost in the fire. Clothes, toasters, blankets, all kinds of practicalities to set up housekeeping were brought.

I was really unsure about bringing one of my own paintings as a gift, so I walked into a classroom with the painting and turned it to the wall. Then I found Janice out on the playground and brought her into the room.

"There is something I want to give you," I said, "because I feel so bad for you since I know how you're grieving."

When I turned the painting around, Janice burst into tears.

I felt so foolish. I thought I should have brought something more practical. Then I put my arms around her and said, "I'm sorry, I didn't mean to make you cry. I should have brought you a toaster or something."

"You don't understand," Janice said, pointing at the painting. "When my home burned down, I only had one thing of my mother's, who has passed away, and it was destroyed in the fire. It is that exact same vase that is in your painting. You haven't given me a painting, you've given me back a part of my mother."

EARLY MORNING VISITOR

Donna Amalong

Donna Amalong, fifty-eight, is an herbalist involved with natural healing and living close to the earth. She lives with her husband, David, on a ranch homesteaded by his family outside of Pearce, Arizona, along Turkey Creek in the Chiricahua Mountains. Firm in their commitment that the ranch will always remain undeveloped property, they have dedicated it to the safety and well-being of all creatures. Eventually they hope to raise wild turkeys and one day release them back into Turkey Creek.

My mother abandoned me when I was about six weeks old. She left me with my great-aunt, Elizabeth Swearingen, who was half Cherokee Indian. My great-aunt was a very spiritual woman, a Seventh Day Adventist who also lived the old religion.

When I was six, my biological mother reclaimed me and took me to live with her and her new husband. After that, my great-aunt, who I called Mom, sustained me through some very ugly times. She was more of a mother to me than my biological mother ever was.

Mom and I were together all of the time after I was grown. We started every day with a telephone call to one another. Mom sometimes talked in rhymes, like

I'm doing nothing
Just like the little rock on the hill

Doing nothing
But sitting still.

She was truly my best friend.

When I was pregnant, Mom knew I would have a girl. After my daughter was born, I named her after Mom, although she made me promise to never call her Lizzie. To ensure that that never happened, I named my daughter Beth instead of Elizabeth.

Mom died twenty-three years ago when she was eighty-five. She'd had minor surgery and died of a staph infection she'd gotten in the hospital. She was in a coma and I'd been visiting her. I left and she died an hour later.

I was absolutely devastated. For days, I was paralyzed with grief; I didn't think I was going to be able to go on. She wasn't there for me to call or to talk to.

One day at five in the morning, two weeks after her death, the doorbell rang. I went to the door, opened it, and there was Mom. She was fifty-six when I was born, so I'd never known her as a young woman, yet she appeared much younger than I had ever known her.

"What are you doing here?" I asked. "You're dead."

"I know," Mom said, "but I need to talk to you."

She came in, sat on the couch, and began to lecture me. "Donna Clyde, stop this. You have two children who need you. You have to get over this and pull yourself up by your bootstraps. I'm having a good time."

I was stunned.

"I want you to dig up the gladiolus at my house and plant them here," she added.

She stood. "I have to go now."

We hugged and kissed and she went out the front door, exactly the same way as she had come in.

My husband came into the living room. "Who was that?" he asked. He'd heard the doorbell and the conversation but he hadn't gotten dressed in time to see who it was.

Mom still comes in periodically as I need her.

When my daughter Beth was pregnant with her first baby, I was crocheting a dress for the baby, who I intuitively knew would be a girl. I was frustrated because I couldn't remember the broomstick stitch pattern that Mom had taught me. I threw down the dress and needles and said, "Damn it, Mom, if you were here, you'd show me."

I went outside and was working in the garden when I heard her laugh and she said, "Pick up the knitting noodles." This was her pet term for the needles. I went inside and picked them up and completed the dress, instantly remembering the forgotten stitch.

Later, when I sent Beth the dress, I included a letter and signed it "Mom." I wasn't even aware that I had done that, because my children up to this point had always called me Mommy, never Mom.

After she received the letter and the dress, Beth called me and mentioned that I had not only signed the letter "Mom," but I'd done it in my mom's handwriting. She thought that was very spooky. However, after that, both of my children began calling me Mom, and I'm Mom to this day.

Sometimes I hear Mom laughing, especially if I'm doing something she liked. She also laughs when she knows that I am frustrated. If I need her, all I have to do is say, "Mom, I need you," and I have the answer.

Her presence is never far away.

SHIFT CHANGE

Dee Beckman

Now retired, Dee Beckman, sixty-three, worked as a medical secretary and also managed a metaphysical bookstore. Originally from Montana and Colorado, Dee plays the cello, sings in a university chorus, and volunteers in a hospital nursery.

For several years I have volunteered in the newborn nursery of a local hospital. One day, about two years after the passing of my mother, I arrived at the hospital for my shift.

As I walked among the cribs of the newborns, I became aware that each time I approached one particular baby girl, she became restless, mewling and fussing in her sleep, although not actually waking up. After this happened several times, I decided to sit and rock her for a while.

She was an adorable baby girl, around seven pounds, with a smooth cap of dark hair and a sweet face. As I became comfortable with her in the rocking chair, tucking her soft little head against my neck, I could actually feel the tension leave her body. She relaxed completely and was in a deep sleep almost immediately.

As I sat there, eyes closed, lightly massaging her little back through her blanket, enjoying her softness against my neck, I was also aware of a very special energy flowing between us.

After sitting with her for a long time, I very gently returned her to her crib, tucking her blanket around her. As I stood there taking a last look at her, a tiny little voice within me said, "She is your mother."

Suddenly I was flooded with an intuitive, quiet inner knowing as a prickly feeling overcame me.

Because I believe in reincarnation, I just stood there for several moments frozen with goose bumps

YELLOW ROSES LEFT BEHIND

Carolyn Niethammer

Carolyn Niethammer, fifty-six, writes about Indians, cooking, and edible wild plants—sometimes all in the same work. Her latest book is *I'll Go and Do More: Annie Dodge Wauneka, Navajo Leader and Activist*. Carolyn lives with her husband in Montclair, New Jersey.

Since my mother and father died, I have felt communications from both of them, but particularly from my mother.

When I was young, my mother and I were very close. However, I reached young adulthood in the turbulent era of the late sixties and early seventies. My involvement with the hippie culture was rather moderate, but to her eyes I was overthrowing all of Western civilization, and we became estranged.

After a few years we were reunited, but I was tense in her presence because I felt she didn't understand me and I had to be on guard. Over time, as I matured and married a man she felt was a fine, upstanding citizen, the relationship mellowed again.

I admired her toughness of character during her first bout with breast cancer. Instead of succumbing to self-pity, she simply said, "I'd much rather lose a breast than an arm," and she went on with her life. When she became ill with a recurrence of her cancer and the subsequent weakening from chemotherapy, I was happy to be able to spend weeks in my parents' home helping my father to care for her. I also became closer to my father during this time, and I admired his devotion to her.

I had hoped to help her die at home, but as she became weaker she decided it would be easier on all of us if she went to the hospital. As she lost strength, she never lost her personality or her sense of humor. We spent most of the day with her and kept her part of the family.

At one point my father mislaid a favorite cap and was grousing about it. In our family my mother had always been the "finder of lost things," and she chafed that she was not home to help hunt for the hat. When she was only a few days away from death and very weak, I was asking her what she wanted and leaned my ear close to her lips to hear her. She said, "I want to help Dad find his hat."

My mother died in my arms shortly after noon one day. That evening my Dad and I went out to dinner with relatives. When we got home, he walked to the hall closet, reached up to a shelf, and pulled down his lost cap. It was clear that as soon as Mom was sprung from that hospital bed, she retrieved the hat.

Later in the evening, after Dad had retired, I was sitting in the darkened living room and I felt her presence there. I knew somehow that she was in the room with me, but it did not feel right. So I told her that she needed to go and that we could cope.

Four years later my father died.

Shortly after that, I was planning to make a trip to the small town where my parents lived and wanted to stop by the cemetery where their ashes are buried side by side. I do not actually believe they are there, but I felt a need to abide by the societal convention of decorating the tiny grave.

On the afternoon before I was going, I stopped to do a

number of errands on my way home from work—buying cosmetics at one spot, groceries at another. My last stop was at a store with a good selection of silk flowers. I planned to buy some yellow roses, my mother's favorite. As I wandered the aisles of the store looking for the perfect thing, I heard her voice clearly: "Really, honey, this isn't necessary. Don't bother." Well, I wanted to look like a good daughter to whoever might come out to that cemetery, so I continued to choose the flowers and wait in line at the cash register although her words kept ringing in my ear. When my purchases were rung up, I went to my wallet to pay, and found that I had used my last check and spent my last cash. The store didn't take credit cards for purchases under fifteen dollars. The flowers went back on the shelf, and I learned that my deepest beliefs are true: What is left of my mother and father is in my heart and not in the cemetery.

Most recently in contemplating a cross-country move, I considered selling my mother's heavily flowered china service in order to buy something more to my taste once I reached my new home. However, as the years have passed, I have fewer and fewer things of hers. Would I be weakening the tie, diluting what remained to the memories? I dithered about what to do until her voice, unexpected and unbidden, came through clearly one day: "Sell it. Don't be silly. Get what you want." I packed up the plates, bowls, and cups, the matching gravy boat and platters, and sold them to an antiques dealer.

A number of years after my father had died, I was in an automobile accident. Someone who had been up all night drinking and driving his new Porsche rear-ended me as I was driving along a narrow road. My car spun around and landed on its side in a ditch. I turned off the engine, rolled down the window, and climbed out, unhurt except for a three-inch scratch on my leg. I had my seat belt on, but as

I thought back, I felt a greater restraint than that, like arms holding me tight to the bucket seat, and it was absolutely clear to me that I had been held safe by the arms of my angel parents. For years, I could not talk about that incident without weeping.

Today, I know that my mother is never far from me.

THE ENERGY OF HAWKS

Lisa Howells

Lisa Howells, forty-four, is a longtime elementary school teacher who currently trains teachers on the use of technology in the classroom. A practicing astrologer for twenty years, she also gives intuitive readings.

Let's just say that my relationship with my mom was a pretty interesting one. Sometimes I felt like she lived vicariously through me even though I expressed myself in ways she didn't necessarily approve of. She herself was quite lively in her own right. Spunky and gregarious, she didn't hesitate to introduce herself to some stranger she met. Perhaps this is a way I carry forth part of her spirit into the world today.

I was the younger of two children, with a half brother who left home before I can remember. Raised in Connecticut, I grew up with that New Englander attitude, that this was the center of the world. And yet, given my adventuresome spirit and hunger to know more, I ventured out West at the age of nineteen into a new environment and a totally different lifestyle.

Many of my choices in life were difficult for my mother to accept, and she didn't hesitate to make her disapproval known. However, she also made it very clear that although she couldn't accept my choices, she still loved me.

Before she got quite ill, we stayed in close contact, but there was always a gap between us. I often felt that if certain things changed in my life, she would be happier.

In October 1996 my mother was diagnosed with pancreatic cancer. Around Thanksgiving she was due to begin radiation treatments, and so I took some leave time from work and went to stay with her for six weeks. When my father was dying, it was my sister, who always lived close to my parents, who shouldered all the family responsibility. I think my mother was touched that I would put my life on hold to be with her.

It was not easy for my mother and me to spend concentrated periods of time together. Maybe we were a bit too much alike in some ways. In the past, even my best efforts to be supportive or helpful would often result in our having some kind of conflict.

This time it was different. We laughed and cried and talked together with relative ease. I knew some of the shift was due to all my prayers and meditations asking for grace. But there was also a tangible difference in both our energies. After years of doing intuitive readings, I am able to sense energy between people, and during this time there was a very special energy present, one which helped us share openly with one another.

After Mom began the radiation treatments, she quickly became weaker and needed more assistance. This was a woman who did not accept help easily. Yet this time she embraced it with grace. That was one of the many gifts she gave me during her illness and passing. She brought joy and laughter and humor into those cold doctors' offices. Those around her couldn't help but laugh or respond to her in kind.

The next gift came the day I left to return home. I needed to go and get my classroom in order for the new semester. Then I planned to return to Connecticut to spend more time with my mom.

That morning, as I was packing, I began to sob. I had this deep feeling that I would never see my mother again.

Six years earlier my father had died five minutes before I arrived, and so I felt it was important that I be there when my mom passed. Yet as the sadness welled up, there was also a feeling of peace and knowing that I wasn't going to be able to do that.

My sister came in and tried to comfort me, trying to tell me that it would be OK. I just wanted her to leave me alone and let me be with the feelings, as I knew that was just where I needed to be in that moment.

I went in to say good-bye to my mom. I told her I loved her and gave her a hug. She was teary, too, and simply said, "I'm going to miss you."

In that moment I knew she was not just talking about my return trip home. I felt she was telling me how she would miss our lifetime together, but there was also something else in those words.

She was acknowledging me in a way I had never experienced with her before. I was no longer just her daughter Lisa. Instead, I sensed that she also saw me as this loving being that she had shared her life with. There was a sense of equality and connectedness. In that instant, I knew we had come full circle, and that whatever differences we had, had dissolved into love.

After being home for about ten days, I got a call from my sister. She was very upset and worried about Mom being dehydrated. The decision was made to take her to an inpatient hospice where she could get rehydrated and then come back home, as was her wish.

A few hours later my sister called again and said, "I think you need to come." I quickly booked a plane reservation for early the next morning.

Before dawn, I arrived at the airport and headed to the counter. As I stood there waiting for my ticket, I began to hear the mantra of my meditation path being broadcast over the airport sound system. Now I probably would have doubted this experience had it not been for my friend who was standing next to me. As we left the ticket counter, I turned and said, "Did you hear that?" without specifying what it was I had heard. She said she had also heard the mantra.

It didn't dawn on me at the time, but when I called the hospice from Dallas during my layover, they told me my mom had already passed on. When I asked about the time, I discovered that she was passing right at the moment I was purchasing my ticket and hearing the mantra play.

Although I was sad and stunned that I again was not able to be there when one of my parents passed, I immediately knew that my mother was not alone and that everything was perfect. In my heart, I knew that I hadn't really missed her, as we both had gotten everything we needed together in that six weeks we had.

I arrived in Connecticut that same night and stayed alone at my mom's condominium. Although it was a familiar place I had visited for more than ten years, now there was this incredible sense of emptiness. It was absolutely clear that her presence was no longer in the physical space around me.

The next day, I made arrangements to go and view her body for a final good-bye before she was cremated. After the funeral home director left, I talked to her for a few minutes, thanking her for all she had given me.

Through my intuitive work, I can feel energy pass through my hands at times. As I put my hand on my mother's shoulder, I suddenly felt this energy running up my arm, the "living" energy you would feel if someone was alive. It startled me at first and then I realized that she had just come for a moment to see me and give me that final good-bye.

During the memorial service there were stained-glass windows behind the altar. As the minister spoke, two birds flew back and forth together outside the windows. Before Mom had passed, she used to talk about my dad, Robert, coming to visit in the form of a bird. I remember having lunch with her at the beach one day, and this seagull landed on the car and she said, "Hello, Bobby."

Following the service, my sister and I spontaneously mentioned the birds. We both had the same thought. In some magical way, these birds were our parents, together once again.

Shortly after my mother's death, I had a dream about her. In the dream, I was staying at her condo. The bell rang and when I opened the door she was there, coming home from the nursing home. (The year before her death she had been in a nursing home for a couple of weeks to recover from open-heart surgery.) She walked in the door and hugged me. When I woke up the next morning, I could feel the sensation of that hug. Despite her physical absence, she just kept giving me what I needed. I believe each experience I had was to help me reach an inner sense of completion in our relationship.

The completion came later in a more practical way. My partner and I were able to buy a house using some money I inherited from my mother. During the process of signing the final papers, I noticed that they had neglected to put my middle name, Dudley—my grandmother's maiden name—on the deed.

Without warning, my eyes welled up. Not really under-standing why at first, I attempted to explain my response to the woman at the title company. In that moment I real-ized using my middle name was a way of affirming my mother's lineage, her mother's gift passed to her and then on to me.

Finally it was moving day. As the movers arrived to pick up our furniture, there was this raucous, unidentifiable sound. I scanned the yard and noticed three large hawks sitting in a dead tree in front of the old house. In three years of living there, I had never seen a hawk anywhere near the property. I turned to my partner and said, "My mom came to visit and she brought my dad, but I can't figure out who the third one is."

Later that day I realized that the third hawk was my grandmother. She died when I was fifteen and although I hadn't felt strongly connected to her before this, I now felt her to be a part of my life and me.

Through all these experiences there was now a sense of a circle complete and full.

When I first moved into my new home, I'd walk in the dry riverbeds and see the hawks. In time, it's changed. They do not come as frequently; the energy is different.

And now when I see them, most of the time they are just hawks.

MOTHER'S CACTUS

Teresa Jahn

Teresa Jahn, forty-five, is an industrial radiation technician for a nuclear power plant. Married, with three grown children, she enjoys writing poems, making quilts, and crafting stained glass. She lives with her husband, Mike, in Dixon, Illinois.

My mother, Joanne Ireland, loved flowers, and one of her favorite colors was purple. The significance of this will be understood when you read the events of how my mother reached out to touch our hearts after she passed away on September 11, 1997.

Mom was afraid of dying and I wanted so desperately to help calm her fears. I prayed I would find the words she needed to hear. I was amazed at the presence of God that I felt around her death. Everything my mother questioned or was concerned about I was able to find and read to her by simply opening books (some were religious, some were not). The pages that fell open related directly to her questions or fears. This happened not just once or twice, but every single time. It truly amazed me to be a messenger of God's words.

I believe Mom was able to die in peace. She was unable to talk the last few days of her life, so she could not tell me how she felt, but she spoke loud and clear to me the day I got home after her funeral.

When I left home to attend my mother's service, there were no blooms on the Christmas cactus she had given me. When I returned, two days later, it was in *full* bloom. I also have two other Christmas cacti (not from Mom), but they did not have any blooms on them at all. I felt a very warm sensation throughout my body because I knew it was a sign from my mother and that she was at peace. I found that I had tears in my eyes.

We were also touched with my mother's presence in another way.

My mother fed the geese at the cemetery many, many times. I remember vividly how the geese flew over her home as she took her last breath, as if it were a salute to her from them and as if Mom were saying her spirit was free. When we found a final resting place for Mom, it was by the lake where she fed the geese and under a huge tree in the cemetery. After her funeral and prayers at the cemetery, the geese flew overhead at the end of the ceremony, once again honoring her.

Then when we were deciding which headstone we wanted for Mom, we decided the only proper one would be a bench to sit on so we could follow with the tradition of feeding the geese and sharing time with Mom while we could pray and speak to her on the bench-style headstone.

We looked for a few months and nothing stood out as special enough. Then I decided to make one for her. I have made many stained glass pieces through the years, and my mother always loved the things I made. I had never made a bench before, but I was bound and determined to make my mother's bench headstone.

It was made with an inlaid stained glass pattern of wildflowers (of course, some were purple) and hummingbirds. Her name, date of birth, and date of death were done in a mother-of-pearl–type glass (also a favorite of hers). The cement for the bench was a light lavender color.

Underneath the bench we engraved the names of all her children and grandchildren. My children also brought a special trinket that meant a lot to them and added it into the cement before it dried. I wish I had thought of it—I would have had all the grandchildren send me a trinket of theirs to add.

It was a truly special tribute to my mother that turned out especially beautiful, not only to look at but to all our hearts, because it contained so many things that she loved.

When we gathered to place the headstone and say prayers, once again the geese flew over us. It really gave us all goose bumps and filled our hearts with a peaceful calm in knowing Mom's spirit was really within the geese. It was a sign from her that she was really with us as those geese flew overhead three times. I also felt like Mom was saying "Thank you" for the beautiful remembrance of her in the bench made from love. It really was remarkable.

Another thing that happened during this time was that I received a very strong urge to go buy Yvonne, my pregnant daughter, a beautiful nightgown. I couldn't believe how strong this urge was, and I couldn't understand why I was having it. I looked in stores on numerous occasions, but always came home empty-handed. Then suddenly one day there it was, and I knew it was the answer to the urge I had been feeling. It was the nightgown I was supposed to buy—purple and full of flowers! Two of my mother's favorite things! I knew then that this was a gift from Grandma's heart to her granddaughter. I wrapped it up and wrote the words that seemed to come to me. Part of what I wrote is as follows:

We all love you very much and are excited about the new baby to be. . . . I know purple may not be your favorite color, but it was Grandma's favorite color, so hopefully it'll have extra meaning for you. She was very proud of you and she loved you very much, so every time you wear it think of how much love she felt for you and feel her heart wrap around

you and give you a warm hug . . . feel Grandma close
to you on your special day and know that she is with
you. Feel the love of her warmth as she surrounds
you. . . .

My story doesn't end there. The Christmas cactus from
Mother stayed in bloom for seven months, until the first
week in April, 1998, long after the other cacti had had their
season of beauty. The last month or so, Mother's cactus
only produced one bud at a time, but to me it was even
more of a sign that Mom was with us and saying good
morning every day. She was letting us know that she was
with us. The last bloom opened on April 3, 1998, the day
that Joshua, my first grandchild, my mother's first great-
grandchild, was born.

Mother's cactus blooms ceased after that, but I feel in
my heart that she wanted us to know that she was with us
on that very special day, and she told us so by sending us
a bloom on the cactus every day until he was born.

RACE DAY

Sandra Heater, Ph.D.

〜 Sandra Heater, fifty-eight, is involved in the real
estate business and is also a consultant in the field
of eating disorders. She runs competitively at all
distances, both on the track and in marathons, and
is involved in grass-roots politics. Sandra's focus is
on her family and on sports (both as a participant
and a spectator).

I grew up in a small Midwestern town in a close-knit family. Both of my parents were always very supportive of
their three girls and whatever we were involved in. I admired my mother tremendously. An ultimate problem
solver, she was very bright, and very creative, with a
tremendous aesthetic sense and appreciation. She helped
me become as aware of, and as enamored of, nature as I
am. My mother was always positive and upbeat and had a
great love of and interest in sports. She had lots of unusual
things about her for someone who was born in 1905. After
my father died, she spent quite a bit of time with us, and
she was always ready and up for anything.

In October of 1994 my mother suddenly became very
ill and went blind. She was gone in about two weeks. I was
back in St. Joseph, Missouri, at her bedside, and I lived in
the hospital during that time.

The Sunday morning that she died was the morning of
the Arizona Special Olympics Benefit run, known as the
S.O.B. ten-miler. It's the official state ten-mile race that
I've done for years.

Kim, my younger daughter, is quite a runner. She was running in that race and I was sending her positive thoughts and energy. Just about the time we would have heard the starting gun, my mother died. The contrast between picturing the race, with all of the vitality, energy, and health of running, and watching my mother literally breathe her last breath was an interesting, to say the least, juxtaposition of emotions.

The next year, 1995, I did the race once again. It was the day of the first anniversary of my mother's death. I had this little conversation with my mother while I was warming up. I said, "OK, Momma, I can use your help today." I knew then that I felt really good, just as if my mother were enfolding me.

It was the most extraordinary race I've ever run. Ten miles is fairly arduous and it was as if the energy source were different than any I'd ever had in any of my previous one hundred to two hundred races. The energy that particular day was just amazing. I could have run forever. It was as though my mother were pushing me gently and elevating my feet. Running was virtually effortless, and a ten-mile race is not usually effortless. The toil of running just wasn't present that day. The physical involvement was there, but it wasn't burdensome.

I passed my age group nemesis, with whom I've been in friendly and fierce competition for years, at the three-mile marker.

After the race we were talking and she said, "When did you pass me, Sandra? I never saw you."

When you run, you're always aware of who is passing you, who is in front of you, the whole dynamics of the race. In fact, I had passed within an arm's length of her, yet she never saw me. There's no way ordinarily that she wouldn't have responded. I remember that when I passed her, I waited for her to challenge, but it never happened.

As I ran I had these incredible bursts of energy. I went on to set a state record for my age group on that day. I have run some good races and some not so good, but it was a whole different feeling and atmosphere in that race. There's no question in my mind that there was a connectedness that day between my mother and me. I just felt her. I didn't have any nerves, just this wonderful feeling of skimming over the ground. It was as if it was virtually effortless.

My training was as a therapist in the field of eating disorders. My leisure time is spent reading medical journals; they comprise 90 percent of what I read. I'm constantly asking, Can this be analyzed? Can this be quantified? What does the research say? How was it conducted? I'm basically research oriented and very data driven, so this isn't something that I would have been particularly receptive to. But it definitely made an imprint and was very comforting.

I was having a lot of trouble with losing my mother and completing the grieving process. It was a very difficult emotional thing for me to do. Unfortunately, there's no way to rehearse that loss. You feel totally bereft and nothing else quite fills that void.

The funny thing about her being with me in that race was that she wasn't particularly supportive of my running. In fact, she would often send me articles on arthritis and sports-related injuries.

When it comes to an experience like this, it's really a broadside to my natural proclivities, my orientation, and my training. Yet I found it so wonderful—comforting, soothing, and completely reassuring.

I'm not particularly religious, although I like to think of myself as an ethical person and as a caretaker of the environment. So this isn't something I would have expected or been conditioned for. This was a great step toward my healing. It was as if my mother was saying, "OK, I'm here on a different plane or dimension, but I'm connected with you just as always." I found that tremendously reassuring. After that, I could let go of a lot of the real pain and the sore spots caused by grief. I was significantly better.

I found it amazing, this whole thing of my sending thought waves to my daughter the year before while I was with my dying mother and then my mother sending them to me. I think our mind is our most untapped resource. Who knows what would happen if we were willing and able to expend our energies in that area?

Reading other women's stories about their connections with their mothers is a validation for me. When something that is extraordinary and forceful and inexplicable happens on one level, I am reassured that these things do indeed occur. Any time we go into an unknown realm, there's a human need to be reassured that it's all right to be where we are. These are affirmations that what happened to me on that race day was not a figment of my imagination.

ROSES, BLENDERS, AND SERGEANT DUSTLESS'S TREASURES

Isa "Kitty" Mady

Kitty Mady is a herbalist living on a mini-farm in southwest Washington, where she is known as the "herb lady who writes all those letters to the editor." This story is the title chapter from her book *My Mother the Battery Charger and Other Cosmic Contacts*.

The anniversary of my mother's death lingers with the holiday wrap and the tinsel, and once again I feel her energy charging my spirit.

She seems to inspire my thoughts and direct my creativity at this particular time of year, silently affirming all that we didn't share during her lifetime. I can't prove it, I can only feel it, but I love it!

I can always tell when she's here for the holidays, since she announces her presence in a grand manner. Her departure is less dramatic, but she leaves behind lots of food for thought. These tidbits become my insights and inspirations during the reflective time of winter, when I begin writing again.

I first felt her presence one late November around 1982–1983, while traveling. I had stopped at an antiques store in Santa Monica, California, where she last lived, and suddenly felt a propelling force that moved me to buy a rose-colored glass figurine. It was a lovely statue of a gowned woman holding an infant in her right arm and a bouquet of roses in her left. I simply had to have it.

Shortly afterward, at my brother's mountaintop home in Northern California, I was reading in bed one night when a terrific wind came up. The two-story house creaked and groaned on its hillside moorings while the wind howled through the rafters like a hundred moor witches. I wasn't exactly scared, but the thought did cross my mind that we could easily be swept off our foundations and scattered like fairy dust to the valley floor 1,400 feet below. Then I felt my mother's presence and it gave me some comfort. She was directing me to look at the glass figurine, which sat on the nightstand beside my bed.

As I gazed at the statue I began to reflect on the roses in the left hand. To one who studies symbolism and the workings of the subconscious as I do, the left symbolizes the past and the right suggests the future.

Additionally, the rose has been the symbol of the healer for centuries. Since my mother's name was Rose, I sensed she was offering me some healing by helping me let go of her and past agendas, and by focusing my attention on youth. "As in teaching?" I wondered.

The rose-colored glass seemed to be a gentle reminder for this daughter she once called Peter Pan (but hoped would grow up to become a teacher) to look at life realistically and not through rose-colored glasses. After I assimilated this brief lesson in practicality, the wind died down as abruptly as it had begun, and I slept soundly for the rest of the night.

Another time I sensed her presence at 3 A.M. while the rest of the family slept. Again it was just before Christmas. I was sitting by the woodstove in my robe, reading a self-help manuscript I'd been working on and pondering over the validity of my writing. I'd been blending humor, art, and lots of teaching about the subconscious into a manual for helping others develop self-awareness. The work excited me, for slow learner that I am, I've needed similar illustration and imagery myself in order to grasp a point. But would anyone else want to read it? I wondered.

All of a sudden, the blender in the kitchen came to life and I shot out of my chair like a rocket! The experience unnerved me, but as I turned off the machine and returned to my chair I found myself forming the question, "Was that you. Mom? Are you trying to tell me that I'm on the right track?"

Again the blender turned itself on for no apparent reason other than the seemingly cosmic approval of my query. This time I smiled and said, "Thanks, Mom, I got the message!" I also realized then how far apart our worlds had once been, and how much her approval meant to me now.

One year her presence seemed to inspire my involvement with our local farmers' market, where I sell my products. I'm a herbalist and make all sorts of concoctions from the plants around us; I also teach others the way of herbs. This time my mother's approval coincided with a blustery snowstorm during a record cold spell for 1990. It was also during the market's busiest days before the holidays, and each of the vendors was working feverishly to turn out new products before Christmas. When my own creativity level suddenly began to soar (in spite of temperatures in the teens), I knew then that Mom's energy was with me, and my spiritual battery began to feel recharged.

I worked with a passion day and night, turning out tonics and tinctures, creams and salves, aromatic blends and tea blends, dream pillows and cedar pet pillows, pressed-flower pictures and hand-colored volumes of my poetry, all in amazing quantity and in record time. My tables soon spilled over with holiday exotica in a myriad of textures and fragrances that dazzled and tantalized the senses. By the time I'd slowed down enough to comprehend the extent to which my creativity had been pushed, I was exhilarated and exhausted.

My mother's visits are never more tangible than sensing her presence keenly, especially in winter. My most intense thoughts of her that Christmas in 1990 occurred in the backyard while I was burning the last remnants of gift-wrap paper and holiday boxes. It was my first quiet contemplation in weeks, and I found myself thinking about how she used to nudge me to have a little shop one day.

I knew that my farmers' market involvement wasn't exactly what she had in mind then, but I sensed she felt OK about it now. She probably enjoyed the atmosphere and the characters there as much as I did, for she was a character herself—a regal character affectionately called "Lady Rose" by her friends.

Suddenly I saw her as she appeared after her last stroke. She was sitting in her high-backed gold velour chair, which enveloped her tiny frame. Flanking her throne on either side were white wicker flower stands holding royal purple violets. She was heavily medicated, and without the usual meticulous grooming that belied her age, she looked old and drawn. Proud to the end, she was trying valiantly to stay awake and maintain her composure while a steady stream of gift-bearing friends came to pay their respects. It was the last time Lady Rose was to hold court.

As the smoke wafted up from my burn pile, I saw other pictures that were hidden in my memory bank—pictures of her as the original Secondhand Rose, who loved a bargain as much as a cruise.

For twenty-five years she did this amazing clothing act with her cleaning lady, Effie. She sold Effie used designer clothes and furniture donated by the wealthy ladies of her synagogue in Beverly Hills. Effie then sold the goods to her church sisterhood in Watts for rummage sales, repaying Mom with a few dollars each week. Dad drove Effie home with her loot every Tuesday, and both sides made out on the deal. Effie's church prospered and Mom raised thousands for her pet project, a home for asthmatic children in Denver. This was probably my earliest exposure to recycling, and to the concepts of quality and equality (not to mention ingenuity).

I also saw a picture of her as a sickly, asthmatic child growing up in Montreal in a large, poor, immigrant family and longing to go to high school, which wasn't affordable for her widowed mother. Discovering she was self-taught beyond the sixth grade had amazed me, for she was articulate and well read. It also explained her vicarious need for me to go to school (and maybe become a teacher), and to live among people of substance, never knowing want again. This became obvious after her death, when I discovered her treasure cache.

She had secret stashes in every drawer and closet. There were unopened boxes of fancy soaps and perfumes her asthma prevented her from using; expensive costume jewelry and trinkets from her own travels and traveling friends; hand mirrors in several sizes and shapes, some bearing her royal birth sign of Leo; and countless greeting cards from decades past and photographs of faces she would no longer recognize.

I didn't know then that the rose was the traditional sign of the healer, but I did sense the kind of healing each trinket and card had brought her at times when her own health and vitality were waning. During her last days I will never forget becoming aware of the wonderful healing energy that hung about her room like an old friend, unlike the depressing aura of death that I'd been expecting. It filled me with such delight; I actually became enlightened by the experience of liquidating her possessions, most of which I gave to my daughters.

One significant treasure in her collection was a 1951 newspaper photograph of three generations of British queens in black mourning garb at the funeral of King George. Since she'd grown up in Canada, I knew that Mom had a special affinity for the royal family, but I was touched nonetheless that she'd saved this photograph for almost thirty years. I knew I would do the same, for I was also moved by the powerful female energy I saw in the photograph. I sensed she had felt it too and was also tuned into the vibrant energy that lingered in her room and routinely lifted her spirits.

With all those regal symbols around me, I wondered about the incongruity of the most domestic and the most baffling of her collections: a silver and blue metal chalk box that once contained "Sergeant Dustless hexagons—the six-sided chalk that won't roll off the desk." It probably belonged to a teacher once, but now it was filled with buttons and pins. It seemed like a strange collection for one who claimed that her blindness in one eye limited her sewing skills to simple mending. Of course, I knew better, knowing her determination in other areas. She simply preferred coordinating fund-raisers and social gatherings to pursuing the domestic arts.

Yet there was this chalk box filled with tiny pearl buttons from infant garments, oversized buttons from the wide-shouldered coats of the forties, and glass bubbles with intricate designs within. There were insignia buttons, military buttons, and buttons shaped like animals. There were also steel, prewar dressmaking pins, and at least fifty corsage pins from many of the dinner dances where she'd been honored for her charity fund-raising efforts. I kept the pins in lieu of an equal number of engraved plaques and framed certificates. I kept the box too, for it was a designer's treasure trove.

The box gets dumped now and again, sometimes by

children who make short-term button pictures on a wooden tray, and sometimes when I'm working on an art project and need one metallic bronze button with scrollwork. Then the buttons get fondled and remembered as they had been by my mother's hands and probably by her mother before her, giving me a loving energy charge and filling me with warm thoughts of my ancestral spirits.

I still use the dressmaking pins, and the neatest buttons find their way into stitchery collages for family and friends, so I get to see them now and again. The corsage pins are stuck in an old wig stand and rarely used for anything but unsticking a tube of craft glue. When I do see them, my thoughts just naturally shift to my mother, who didn't sew but who left me a priceless chalk box button collection for the day when I would sew, and with it, a reverence for teaching and helping others.

My final visit with my mother that Christmas of 1990 ended when my outdoor burn pile reduced itself to ashes. Without its heat I quickly became aware of the coldness that surrounded me and knew it was time to wind down from the season's activity and my annual supercharge. I also knew I would write about it later, putting it into perspective as I'd done so often since Mom's death, getting in touch now with values she'd tried to share during her lifetime, but which I willfully resisted as a headstrong kid with ideas of my own. With her death she had become my personal moral force for influencing my own future generations.

My mother died on December 8, 1978, the same day as Golda Meir. She'd admired Israel's first lady as much as she admired the Queen Mother, so we thought her departure that day was fitting.

It was after the funeral, during the catered reception we held per her wishes, that an actor friend commented on the poignant humor of the moment: "Golda was probably going to stage this *big* fund-raiser in the sky," he said, "so she took Lady Rose along because nobody could sell more tickets for charity than Rosie, right?"

I knew he was right, for I had the corsage pins to prove it.

SUSANNA, DON'T YOU CRY

Susy Smith

Susy Smith died last year after spending a lifetime writing about the paranormal. She initiated the Susy Smith Project through the University of Arizona Psychology Department. The goal of the project is to prove that there is life after death. Her last book, *The Afterlife Codes*, details this work. The following story was first published in her book *Confessions of a Psychic*.

At Christmas, 1947, my mother gave me a musical powder box that played "Susanna Don't You Cry." But even though it admonished me not to cry, every time I raised its lid and the tinkly tune started, tears came to my eyes because I knew by then that Mother was going to die and hearing that melody always called attention to the fact.

Mother died on the twenty-first of March, 1949, exactly two months before her sixtieth birthday. A heavy smoker all of her life, she had what they then called a "leaky" heart.

My little music box had sat on my dresser for a long time neglected because of the tears it brought when it played. But three weeks later, about four o'clock in the morning, the powder box began to play. I awoke, alarmed, and then was somehow comforted by the strains of "Oh, Susanna, don't you cry for me." Although it momentarily sounded like a direct message from Mother, I almost immediately began to try to figure some natural means by which the lid could have become jarred loose. There were no vibrations in the house; we did not have mice—what other thing could have caused it normally? That I wasn't able to conceive of any possible way it could have happened did not convince me it was anything other than a physical phenomenon free of any supernatural origin. But . . . what you profess to believe and what you secretly hope could be true are two different things. It was consoling at least to consider the possibility that Mother was taking this means to tell me she was still around.

I had been an agnostic all my life until 1955, when I read two books by Stewart Edward White and began to open my mind to the possibility of life after death. I started with *The Unobstructed Universe*, in which White wrote rather compelling evidence that he had communicated with his deceased wife. It presented a concept more inviting than any I'd encountered before and it wouldn't let me alone. It teased me and titillated my thinking, and soon I succumbed to the interest it aroused. I went to the library and got another book by White—*With Folded Wings*.

In that I came upon the statement that our loved ones who have passed on would like to communicate with us to reassure us there is no death and that they are often with us. White said if we will make the first move toward contact, they'll cooperate.

The idea of communication, the way he told it, would be plausible enough, if there were really spirits around. If, as he insisted, our friends were still hovering about, why shouldn't they want us to know it, to relieve our grieving for them if that were the case . . . to assuage their own egos, for that matter, for who would want to be totally ignored all the time? Also, when they became aware of one who was in terror of the gaping void of death, wouldn't they feel an intense desire to say, "Look, it isn't like that at all. I'm still here, you'll be here still, there's more to all this than meets the eye."

Just as a theory, I say, it sounded all right. But I didn't buy it. Still, the chance that it might be possible was enthralling to me. I stopped reading and went outside for a walk with my little dachshund, Junior.

There, on a crisp, sunny afternoon in March, as my dog and I ambled through a large field covered with dried grass and weeds, I was suddenly infused with a warm, loving awareness of Mother's presence. I could have reached out and patted her cheek—she was that close to me. She was as real and as there as she had been the last time I tucked her in for the night . . . or the many long-ago times she had given me my funny old teddy bear to hug and tucked me in for the night.

This was an incredible thing to me, coming just when it did, for I'd never had such a feeling before in all the six years since Mother's death. And life took on an immediate new dimension, which I knew it would never lose. It was a beautifully tender confirmation of the hope for survival; and no matter what happened to me in the future, I would always cherish this experience and be eager if possible to recapture it.

A PICTURE'S WORTH...

Erma Cooke

Erma Cooke is a neonatal nurse practitioner who has spent the last seventeen years working with critically ill to well newborns in a hospital setting. She is also a photographer and a short story writer and a spoiler of her miniature schnauzers, named Joy and Chance. Erma, thirty-seven, lives in Killeen, Texas.

My mother's name was Erma Cooke. She was the youngest daughter of seven children, and I am the youngest daughter of her seven children. I am also her namesake and her sisters enjoy telling me how much I remind them of her.

My mother and I had a special relationship that was strengthened when she was diagnosed with throat cancer when I was only eleven. Breast cancer was diagnosed in her the following year. For the last two and a half years of her life, she could not talk. I learned in those years to communicate without words. We developed an incredible way of "hearing" one another even when we were not together.

I was fourteen when she was dying, and I remember being in school on the many days she was in the hospital or having surgery. I could tell when she went to surgery, how the surgery had gone, and how she was doing post-op.

The morning she died, she stood on the trailer steps and watched my school bus go out of sight. She was waving our special "Good-bye, I love you" wave. One and a half hours later she was dead.

When my sister came to my class to tell me to get my stuff because Dad was coming to get us, I knew my mother had died.

Before Mom died, life was tough for me because my father and I didn't get along. He was a drinker, and violent at times, and Mom had always been our buffer. After she died, I no longer had that cushion to keep me safe in a violent environment. I felt isolated, unloved, and unsupported. Those feelings intensified a year later when Dad sent me away to live with one of my brothers, who was stationed in the army in Germany.

When I returned home two years after Mom's death, Dad had me live in his house while he lived fifty miles away. I was very lonely and hurt that he didn't want me. Although there was always an older brother or sister living there, and while Dad always met my physical requirements, no one seemed concerned about my emotional needs. I don't believe anyone realized how isolated, lonely, and hopeless I felt. I didn't think anyone cared, so I certainly didn't bring it up.

One afternoon during my junior year of high school, I came home from school feeling very alone and unloved. No one was home to greet me or to even know that I was there. I was lying on my bed trying not to think about it when I had the sense that someone was watching me. The house had several doors and someone could have gotten in without my knowing it. We lived out in the country and didn't have many neighbors. I was scared, but I slowly turned over in bed and saw this young woman standing in the doorway to my room. As soon as I saw her this incredible feeling of peace and stillness came over me.

She was dressed in a beautiful white dress, wearing a shiny butterfly necklace, and she was just standing there looking at me. At first I was frightened, but then I somehow knew that she wouldn't hurt me. Not a word was spoken, but peace, love, and contentment filled the room. After a few moments the woman started disappearing from the feet up. From that time on, I knew that I wasn't alone and whoever this woman was, she would always be with me.

Imagine my shock and surprise when, the following summer, I discovered a picture of the woman. I was visiting my mother's sisters and looking through old photo albums of them when they were young. I turned the page and there she was—wearing the same beautiful white dress, butterfly necklace, and hairstyle.

I quickly pulled my hands off the book and asked, "Who is she?"

Her sisters answered, "Why, that is your mother when she was about your age."

I've known since that moment that Mom is with me. She knows my successes and failures, and no matter what, she will always support me.

In June 1999, as I was looking at pictures taken during my commitment ceremony, I noticed a shadow of a woman who had not posed for the pictures. It was wild. I looked through the roll of film looking for defects and I couldn't find any.

My partner was showing off the pictures, and a friend who knew nothing of my mom looked at it and asked her who the person with long dark hair and a white dress was. My partner said no one. Later she told me about it and I told her the story of my mom visiting.

We just smiled.

LIFE AFTER LIFE

Victoria Houston

Victoria Houston, the author of the Loon Lake fishing mystery series, lives in northern Wisconsin. Her five nonfiction books include the recently coauthored *Restore Yourself: A Woman's Guide to Reviving Her Libido and Passion for Life*. In her spare time Victoria can be found hunting and fishing.

My mother, Alice McBride Kirsch, died of a heart attack sometime during the night of January 16, 1978. She was just short of her fifty-sixth birthday and had lived with multiple sclerosis for over thirty years. A funny, optimistic woman, she was also quite psychic—sensing when people were ill, were coming to visit, were going into labor—a touch of which I've perhaps inherited. But those are other stories. This is the story of her death and her life after that.

Just before she died, the Christmas holiday found me living in Kansas City and standing in my mother-in-law's kitchen, enthralled with a conversation I was having with my sister-in-law who was visiting from California. Janet had just read the Raymond A. Moody book *Life After Life*. For an hour I listened to her description of what she had read about near-death experiences. I found it fascinating.

About a week or so later, I had a dream. In my dream, I was in the living room of the house I had grown up in, in northern Wisconsin. The room was empty of furniture and I was sweeping away dust balls when my father rolled a gurney in. On it lay my mother. He told me she was dying and it was my turn to say good-bye.

I didn't know what to say. Then I remembered every word Janet had told me and I repeated her stories to my mother. I stressed that it was easy to die, according to all the near-death experiences reported in the book. I described the light she would see, the person who would welcome her. I reassured her that death was easy.

My father came back into the room and told me my time was up. End of dream.

I sat bolt upright in my Kansas City bed, stunned.

A few days later, my mom called just to say hi. This was unusual as we were not "mother-daughter buddies" and she rarely called me on the phone. As we talked, I could not get the dream out of my head. She ended our chat with the words "I love you." That was something she did not say. I hung up the phone feeling very strange.

So I wasn't surprised when I got a call within a few days from one of my brothers, telling me that my mother had died. They didn't know exactly when but they found her in the bathroom. I happened to be sick with a bad cold when that call came, but I made a plane reservation and got ready to fly north immediately. My husband and children were not going to come along. I drove myself to the airport, stopping to buy a black skirt for the funeral and pick up a copy of *Life After Life*.

All I did on the flight north to the little town where I'd grown up was read that book. It was reassuring. My father met my flight and as we drove to town he asked me to plan the Mass with our old family friend and Roman Catholic priest Father Gleason. My dad and Father Gleason had grown up together.

A short time later, Father Gleason and I sat in the kitchen alone together. He said that after saying Mass he would like to tell some of my mother's favorite jokes—jokes that she told, even if they were a little off-color. "Great," I said.

And then he asked me if I would mind if he did a reading from "a secular book." I shrugged, unsure what he could possibly mean.

"I would like to read from a little book called *Life After Life*," he said.

And that is when I knew that my mother had heard me. That she had loved me. And that she was all right.

Two things have happened in the years since my mother's death. I had another dream shortly before my father was nearly killed in a car accident. In that dream, my mother appeared living in a very nice brick home, much nicer than our childhood home, and doing my father's wash. I was concerned because he had remarried since her death—so I hesitantly mentioned that he didn't need her to do his shirts. "I know that," she said calmly, "but he's coming for a visit." And indeed he was.

A short time later my father was in a serious car accident. Suffering from severe head injuries, damage to one of his legs, and a crushed foot, he was on life support for forty-eight hours. Hovering between life and death, there was no certainty he would live. He was in a coma for several days before he finally came out of it.

The other event is the writing of this brief memoir. Sinclair Browning suggested I write this months ago. I kept putting it off—on deadline with a book, on deadline with the holidays. Today I finally sat down to write.

As I typed in the first line with the date of my mother's death, I realized today is January 16. Today is the anniversary of her death.

Is this an accident?

I am at a point in my life when I need to be reassured

that I have made the right choices. I feel with all my heart that this is the sign that I have been looking for—in dreams and in daily life. That I chose to write on this date is my mother telling me that I will be all right.

SOUL BIRDS

Linda Gray

Linda Gray, fifty-eight, was born in Amarillo, Texas. She wears many hats, including designing and making rain gauges and yard art, is an ice vendor for a small mountain village, and runs a dog boarding kennel. She also has a Christmas tree farm and is a part-time real estate agent.

Growing up in the forties and fifties, my experience of the world consisted of the panhandle of Texas, where we lived, and west Texas, where we had family. If the world was not flat, I did not know that. Everywhere I looked, I could see forever. It looked flat.

I lived with my father, my mother, a younger sister, and a dog. Later into my childhood, we added a baby brother. Life was a bowl of cherries—even the pits did not pose many problems.

My mother, among her many roles, was the energetic force directing much of the creativity and the fun. She could cut and sew a coat or a schoolgirl's costume, plant and tend a garden, write a letter, sing to a baby, give a home perm, talk on the phone, play bridge, lead a Girl Scout troop, minister to a sick child, organize a picnic on the creek of Palo Duro Canyon, and fry the chicken before we left home, always looking like a million dollars, and, it seemed, all at the same time, wearing high-heeled shoes.

Daddy built roads, so most of the time he worked out of town during the week, which left Mother to handle whatever came up at home. She made the best of it; then weekends with Daddy home were like celebrations for all of us. Family, friends, home, and church must have rewarded Mother with creative energy, refilling her cup with the love she gave away all the time.

Several years after I married and had two little girls, we moved our young family to Arizona. Mother was never as far away as the miles between us. She always kept in touch, sending letters, surprises, and gifts through the mail all through the years. Her granddaughters grew up with her love an active part of their lives, and she always had them come to Texas in the summer.

There were times throughout the years when we needed her help. She always came when we called, bringing her own joyful presence as well as her tender loving care to see us through.

So it was a shock when she was suddenly gone from this world.

We were building a Santa Fe home at the time and had traveled to northern New Mexico for materials and were staying with friends.

After dinner the telephone rang. It was our priest, a family friend, calling with the darkest news in the blackest of nights.

The dark hours passed in tearful disbelief, in anguished prayerful pleading for something, yet nothing specific that I can recall. However, an answer came with a dawn I shall never forget.

Awake through the black night, I opened my eyes to an amazing surprise in the first light of morning. As I looked out the bedroom window toward the colorful bluffs of the Santa Fe countryside, a big cloud appeared just outside the window. There was not a cloud in the sky except that one—a bright glowing, orange color, my mother's color. Instantly I knew, somehow I knew, the cloud was there to tell me, "She's all right. Your mother is here with Me now, in My gentle care forevermore."

The memory of that bright cloud and its message helped me face each day of those early painful months of grief. I began to seek relief in a search for spiritual understanding, mostly through books and articles, including daily Bible reading. What had previously been somewhat of a sporadic curiosity, had now become an earnest, wholehearted search for the eternal, for a lasting reality that the world had not provided.

Much to my surprise, during a routine morning reading, I read about a "bright cloud" that sounded so very much like the one I had experienced. The bright cloud appeared in Matthew's story of the transfiguration. In the scene are descriptions of the mountain and the bright cloud, characteristic of revelation scenes.

Only a few months after her death, a butterfly, the first of what I've come to think of as "soul-birds," made an appearance. On a summer mountain picnic, we were sitting on a log in the forest with a couple of our bird dogs. At first it was just a butterfly. I'd seen them many times and was always fascinated by their bright colors and gentle movement. This one, though, hung around all during our picnic—hovering over me, sitting on my shoulder or shoe or knee. The butterfly had my attention and before long I had a real sense of my mother's presence, and it felt good for her to just drop by and say "hi."

A few weeks after this first encounter, my teenage daughter came home from high school with an interesting story. She was sitting at her desk in class that day when a very attentive butterfly danced all around her face, landed on her shoulder, then flitted to the top of her head. It seemed that as soon as she had her granddaughter's rapt attention, plus all the other students noticing her, she floated out the open window of the classroom.

I loved hearing her story and began to share my own, and what it had meant to me. My daughter perhaps already knew, and my story just reminded her. We were of the same mind about butterflies after that.

There were occasional attentive butterflies during the next several years. One in particular is etched in my memory. On a wonderful trip to South America, I took a side trip to Iguazú Falls, truly one of the natural wonders of the world. Part of touring the falls takes you along wooden sidewalks over the river, and there's also some jungle adventure.

When a butterfly attached to me and stayed with me several times during the hours of the tour, I was really impressed and thrilled that travel was now so easy for Mother. I introduced my butterfly to another woman on the tour and told her about the profound meaning it had for me. Several years later, on another trip with the same group, the woman reminded me about the butterfly that had found me on that other continent. She told me that she had never forgotten what I had shared with her, and that she thought about it from time to time.

Mother had touched both of us that day at Iguazú Falls. Somewhat of an irony, but years before her death, Mother had some butterflies framed in glass and she commented that she really didn't like butterflies very much. It seemed sort of strange at the time, but now it seems somewhat amusing.

From the first time I had visited the mountains as a child, it was hard to imagine why we lived where the world was so flat. After all, there were other choices. Dreams of a cabin in the mountains began early in my life.

A few years after the first grandchildren arrived, that dream came true and my husband and I began building a mountain home. Moving on site to the beautiful property, I spent the summer with a construction crew creating a log cabin. To furnish the new house, I ordered unfinished pine furniture. My big project was to sand and put coats of finish on all the furniture. On a sunny autumn mountain morning outdoors as I was grinding away with the electric sander, I couldn't help but notice a somewhat pesky hummingbird circling me as I worked.

It was delightful to have hummingbirds on the property, but this one was behaving differently than any I had seen before—buzzing, circling, diving, wheeling all around me as I continued sanding the furniture. All of a sudden, recognition came to me and I heard myself saying out loud, "Good morning, Mother."

As I said it, I was laughing with a joy from deep within. With such clarity it hit me. This is exactly like something my mother would be doing, and loving it. Of course she'd want to be here with me to share this. It made perfect sense that mountain morning, and I continued to feel her presence. The pine furniture is still beautiful, and because of that morning, it reminds me of her. Soon after, as winter approached, we and the hummers all left for warmer climates.

As soon as we arrived each summer after that, a few hummingbirds would start buzzing around the cabin, chattering loudly, actually fussing, until I would fill the feeders with syrup and hang them. Their obviously excited welcome became a special, if noisy, part of opening the cabin each summer. Word gets around quickly, and on occasion, there would be fifty or sixty hummingbirds using the feeders, all at once.

One summer, my godparents, Pat and Eleanor, came from Texas to visit me at the cabin for a few precious days. They were my mother and father's lifelong friends, and have always been very important in my life.

One morning, as Eleanor was sitting on the sofa near the window, I noticed a hummingbird hanging around the window for an unusually long time, as if it were really taking time to look in the cabin. I had never seen one do that before. I wondered if it was because Eleanor was there. She and Mother had been young brides, young mothers, and young grandmothers together, sharing the vicissitudes of life all through the years.

Later, Eleanor was sitting by the dining room window, and I saw a hummingbird right outside that window, dancing with wings and watching. In those few days of their visit, it seemed wherever Eleanor was in the cabin, a hummingbird would appear and watch her. Once again I sensed my mother's presence. Of course Mother would want to be a part of this visit.

Nothing like that had happened before, nor has it happened since.

Sometimes our lives move in directions we cannot anticipate. And so it was with my divorce. A few summers ago I moved permanently to the cabin in the mountains, alone. Accepting the death of my thirty-five-year marriage, I experienced a deeper grief than I could ever have imagined. While I was away one week that summer, a friend stayed in the cabin.

When I returned, Carol had a story to tell me. She told me that a hummingbird had been inside the cabin, flying all around. She thought it was frightened, tired, and lost. Gently picking it up, she put it outside. She said as she picked it up, it was semiconscious, and as she laid it on the pedestal of the Saint Francis statue on the porch, she heard it breathe two soft little sighs. Soon it recovered and flew away.

When my response to her story was, "Carol, that was my mother," she looked surprised but immediately I could tell she understood, and she loved hearing the rest of the story. It was very comforting to me to hear that mother had come inside the cabin that particular summer.

The following autumn my firstborn daughter was moving into her new home, her dream house. She had not only planned it, but had also acted as the general contractor during the construction. During the move-in, a hummingbird flew inside, flying all over the house, as if wanting to see all of it. My daughter was able to catch it and release it outside. She had heard enough of my stories through the years to sense that this was something her grandmother did not want to miss.

My sister tells of receiving hummingbird feathers in an envelope, through the mail, on several occasions, from her son. Spending many summer months in the mountains during his years growing up, my mother's grandson seems to attract hummingbirds just wanting to be caught, and a few feathers would always stay on his hand. For some reason, he would mail them to his mother.

There was only one more butterfly incident worth noting, many years after the first hummingbird visit. Several of us were planting petunias in an old potty sitting under some trees on the mountain property. We were having such a silly good time when a butterfly appeared, obviously wanting to join the fun. She darted and swooped around faces, sitting on shoulders, floating all around us until the flowers were planted. Then she left.

If I dare to speculate on such mysterious matters, the transition from butterfly to hummingbird is understandable. Knowing my mother, the high energy and dynamics of the hummingbird reflect her personality more closely than a slowly floating butterfly. The hummingbird moves fast, reportedly beats its wings at a top-speed rate of two hundred beats per second. There are those today, following ancient tradition, who believe that hummingbirds possess magical powers of love. Hummers fly wild and free, capable of extraordinary acrobatics. However, one has never been known to manage to soar on motionless wings.

Did Mother have to learn to float slowly and gently, to silently and softly soar as a butterfly before she could take off to greater heights? On reflection, I can't help but wonder, does the hummingbird signify a graduation?

On my birthday just past, I had another touching serendipity. Each morning I spend at the mountain cabin begins with looking out the window toward the forest, in quiet meditation. I saw a hummingbird appear at the window, strangely staying in one position as I watched, treading air with fluttering wings, it seemed.

As I gazed intently, moved by a feeling of Mother's presence on my birthday, I realized its thin little beak was poking into the window screen, thus the stationary position. While I was trying to decide whether to enjoy the proximity of my celebratory hummingbird or to step outside and free it, she suddenly pulled out of the screen and flew on. I had received a wonderful birthday greeting.

In the last few years since I have put pen to paper to tell about my mother's afterlife gifts, my family has been faced with great personal losses. I sought counseling to help me heal the grief.

My counselor's office was filled with hummingbirds, depicted in various art forms. I shared with him my writing of this story, "Soul Birds." After he told me he liked it, I shared my concern that I might have ruined future appearances by writing about my mother's afterlife gifts. I was disappointed that it had been a long time since I had recognized my mother's spiritual presence.

He said, "Perhaps your awareness served the purpose like a recurring dream. Once you get the message, you no longer need to have the dream."

As I processed his suggestion, I felt better. It fit.

That very afternoon, as I was sitting on my porch a hummingbird flew to a potted geranium. As I noticed the tiny bird, in a matter of seconds I was aware of Mother's presence. At the moment of recognition, she flew away.

So I had not ruined anything. In her own way, she let me know how important it is that I continue to honor these experiences by sharing them.

WAIKIKI LANE AND HIDDEN TREASURE

Kathy Vasquez

Kathy Vasquez lives in a small town in Utah.

My mother and I had a really close relationship. She taught me about birds and bird-watching, and we both collected the same kinds of things, including wheat pennies and mercury dimes.

Four years after her death, a week before I left for Hawaii for vacation, I dreamed of my mother. She was in my kitchen, with a hand-drawn map, urgently telling me to look and listen as she pointed and explained. In my dream, I didn't understand what she meant.

My second night in Hawaii I got lost because a street sign was turned around. I was in a dangerous area. My car was stopped at a corner and hoodlums were wandering toward it. Confused, I couldn't decide which way to turn. Suddenly the dream came back to me and I saw the map clearly in my mind and heard my mother's voice telling me to take the narrow lane.

As I looked, I could see that it was overgrown with tall weeds and apparently no longer in use. I questioned it, thinking, *What if I run over glass and get a flat tire?* Afraid, I somehow knew that it was better than being stuck in that dangerous neighborhood.

So I took it and that got me back onto the main road. I learned later from my aunt, that my mother, who had been born in Hawaii, lived in that district more than forty years earlier. She had walked down that particular lane—the old Waikiki Lane—many times, to go to the shops in town.

Mother was also very intuitive. I remember being very sick at school one day. We had no phone and the school nurse was getting ready to call our neighbors when my mother suddenly appeared. "I had such a bad feeling," she said. "Are you all right?"

When I was growing up, she'd tell me not to go on certain dates because she had bad feelings. While I was never sure whether she was being manipulative or not, I always followed her advice. Once we discovered that one of my potential dates had robbed someone. "I told you I had a bad feeling about that boy," she said. Today I have similar feelings with my own kids.

Before she passed away, I also intuitively knew that my mother was very sick.

In early 1983, when the doctor told her she didn't have long to live, she brought a box to my house and told me to keep it secret from her estranged second husband. When she walked out, she said, "He'll never lay hands on my valuables."

After she passed away, my stepfather complained to me that someone had stolen certain documents and valuables from him. He was getting a court order to have my place searched and possibly have me arrested if anything was found in my house. So I gave him the box my mother had left with me.

Two years later he gave it back to me because he was moving. He said he never did find what he was looking for.

One night six years later, I was going through the box. I couldn't see what was so valuable about any of it—a couple of *Reader's Digest* pamphlets, a Bible, an empty wallet with business cards in the clear plastic sleeves, a head scarf, and things like that. I was thinking of throwing it all away.

I'd spent too much time going through the box and needed to go to work in four hours, so I dumped it in the kitchen trash and went to bed, feeling sorry for my mother that she had lived such a frugal life as to consider those meager things her "valuables."

I was awakened with the urgent sensation I'd get as a child when my mother was scolding me to get out of bed before I'd miss the school bus. As I jumped up, I swear I smelled coffee in the kitchen and the clicking sounds of silverware as though my mother were there. I was confused. Then, on my way out of the kitchen, I looked in the trash.

There was money sticking out of a magazine and out of the Bible pages. I gathered up quite a lot of cash and then got ready for work.

Exhausted from my lack of rest, I fell asleep at the kitchen table, waiting for my ride. Waking to a honking horn, I was so startled that I was clumsy and ran into the trash can. The trash spilled on the floor, so I stuffed it all back in the can and ran. But on my way out, l stumbled on the wallet, which had slid into the living room. I picked it up and decided to save it for sentiment.

The next day, I felt an urgent need to take the business cards out of the wallet and put my kids' pictures in their place. I saw that my mother really meant it before she died, when she said her husband would never get his hands on her valuables. Because she had hidden them in between the business cards in that wallet!

There, I found very valuable silver certificates that she had bought before World War II.

FOUR GENERATIONS OF EXTENDED LOVE

Jo "Sky" Sawyer-Roof

Jo "Sky" Sawyer-Roof, fifty-nine, is the assistant editor of a professional journal as well as an artist whose mixed-media work includes oil and acrylic paintings, drawings, sculpture, and ceramics. Her hobbies include dancing, music, singing, and the theater.

The last time my mother, Virginia, saw her mother, Josephine shared a special secret with her. She knew the pain her daughter was suffering in watching her prepare to leave, and instructed Mother to gather together all of the ingredients necessary to make biscuits and to bring them to her deathbed.

My mother did not understand, but did as she was instructed. She found that the activity helped to distract her aching thoughts.

"The secret of light biscuits is that they must be mixed by hand," my grandmother said. "Mix love into them from your heart."

As tears welled in her eyes, my mother made the dough. Josephine patted her hand, and said, "Do not be sad. I promise you, you will be compensated for this loss."

My grandmother, Josephine Davis, died that day, and the whirlwinds of time moved her promise into the past.

* * *

After having been told they would never have children, and being barren for ten years, my parents had three babies in a five-year period.

During this time, in the middle of the night, the desperate voice of my grandmother Josephine awoke my parents. They sat bolt upright and stared at each other in confusion, for they had each heard the clear words calling out, "Virginia! The baby!"

When they scrambled to the crib, they found their healthy, strong second son, my older brother, Donald Lee, turning blue. He had gotten tangled in a blanket that had wrapped around his neck.

Sent to his bedside by the call of his grandmother, my parents were able to save their small son's life. What was even more surprising is that Josephine Davis, the grandmother who had awakened them that night, had died before her grandson was born. Now Virginia and Speedy Sawyer knew she had not only met their son but was with them, watching over their children.

My parents had been elated with the birth of their daughter, Barbara Marion, and certain now that they had a girl, their family was completed. Not so!

When I was placed into my mother's arms, she recalled her mother's dying words, for in my eyes she felt recognition as she looked into the features of her beloved mother. They named me Jo, after my grandmother.

Although I'd never met her, I became much like my namesake, whom I came to think of as my invisible mentor. Many of my mother's family seemed drawn to me because of my uncanny likeness to my grandmother Josephine. In sharing their secrets with me, I felt their love.

In time I married and had a son and a daughter.

After they were grown, my husband and I decided to make a trip we'd been dreaming about come true. We were concerned about my mother, Virginia, who lately had been weak and strangely tired. But after assurances that things were fine, we left for our dream cruise through Alaskan waters.

The first day on the ship I was eating dinner with a group of new shipboard friends when a strange sensation came over me. I stopped talking in midstream, my fork frozen in midair.

"What is it?" my husband asked.

I knew what had happened. I swallowed hard and said quietly, "It's my mom, she just stopped by to say hello . . . and good-bye." My mother had died. I knew it and exchanged a knowing glance with my husband.

After the meal we were paged to the ship-to-shore telephone. The phone call confirmed what I already knew. My mother had simply closed her eyes and died.

I knew Mom would want me to remain on the Alaskan cruise, and, after some debate, we made that choice. The other passengers were aware of my loss, and when asked, I told them stories of Mother's heralded life of giving and love for others.

I would end each account with a comment such as, "I know my mom. She is in some heaven someplace out there, busier than ever. Probably loving every moment. I'm sure of it."

At the end of the cruise I was surprised because many people thanked me for the way I had handled my mother's death in such a beautiful way. As for me, I thought of my mom and how even in death she had taught others about life, and found there was room only for joy.

My mother also said good-bye to her three-year-old great-grandson, Bryan. Born with his umbilical cord wrapped three times around his tiny neck, he was another miracle baby for our family.

On the morning after my mother's death young Bryan woke up all smiles. "Daddy," he told his father, Derric, "I saw Great-Grandma last night, and she was beautiful!"

On earlier occasions Bryan had spoken of dreams he had had of me, so Derric thought he was having another one. "You mean Grandma, don't you?" he asked.

"No, I saw Great-Grandma," the child was definite in his response.

Derric pressed his son, for he knew the woman had died the previous night. "Tell me where you saw her."

"We were at Aunt Barbara's house," Bryan responded. "Uncle Don and Aunt Mil were there, but no one saw us. They didn't even know we were there!"

Derric was stunned. The child was right, although he hadn't known that his Uncle Don and Aunt Mil had flown in to be with my failing mother. Derric was thus assured that his small son had truly experienced his great-grandmother's presence.

Every night for a week, Bryan related visits with his great-grandmother. Mornings upon awakening he would casually tell his father simply that "Grandma said to say hello."

Once Bryan stopped recounting the visits, we assumed that my mother had settled into her new surroundings and had simply gotten busy. The nightly visitations of Bryan's great-grandmother were left to the recesses of the mind and in time were forgotten.

Eighteen months after Bryan's birth, another son, Alex Michael, joined the family.

Three years after that, one night in January, I awoke to the realization that I had been chatting with my mother for the entire night. It was real. It had not felt like a dream at all. I did not take mental notes of my surroundings. Instead I centered upon all the things I wanted to talk to my mother about. I told her family news and shared secrets of the years since she was away. And what I remember most was that Mom was as beautiful as Bryan had described her. She seemed content and was in perfect health. Things were going well with her.

It felt wonderful, and I was elated when I awoke.

But suddenly the phone rang. My daughter-in-law Debbie, young Bryan's mother, had gone to the hospital to deliver her third child. The baby was in trouble. The umbilical cord had dried up and he was arriving early.

Speaking of the experience later when their new son was safely home, Derric and Debbie both said that the obstetrical nurse who assisted them during that long day not only looked like but acted like my mother, Virginia, who had died years earlier. The presence of this gentle soul was a great comfort to both of them, and they accepted her as a precious gift.

This may have been a coincidence, for the family has no way of confirming whether the hospital staff had a woman working that day who answers to Virginia Davis Sawyer's description. Perhaps it was an angel who had stepped over for a day to greet a new great-grandson, Garric Christopher, and calm the nerves of a beloved grandson and granddaughter-in-law.

After all, it was the anniversary of her birth date. Garric Christopher was born January 9, 1990, and Virginia Mae Davis was born on January 9, 1909. A simple reversal of two numbers. If it was she, we say simply, "Thanks. Thanks for coming."

And so we have through the generations a love that expands. May it continue forever.

SOMEONE TO WATCH OVER ME

Phyllis Hawkins

Phyllis Hawkins, fifty-five, was born in her mother's home in South Carolina while her father was in Europe during World War II. She came to Arizona when she was only eighteen months old, lived briefly on the White Mountain Apache Indian Reservation, and grew up in Winslow, Arizona. She is the CEO of a legal recruiting firm.

I am by nature a skeptic. I will believe there are UFOs when I see one. I eschew tarot card readers and those obsessed with astrology. But so many things—some small, some of extraordinary importance—have happened in the life of our family that cannot be explained by mere chance.

My mother had an unerring sense about people. When I was a teenager, she scrutinized my dates and boyfriends like a hawk. We had a system: I would delay getting ready and she would sit with the young man in her kitchen. She could cross-examine like Clarence Darrow. If she sensed the slightest problem, she would send us out the door with a curfew that left little room for hanky-panky. If she liked the young man, she would be more flexible.

My husband of thirty-two years and I grew up in the same small Arizona town, but we did not date until late in our senior year of high school. He had something of a reputation for being wild and fast, so I was apprehensive when he asked me out. Our system would back me up, however; my mother would figure this guy out right away, so I accepted.

When he arrived at the appointed hour, I was, per the plan, "late" getting ready. As I dallied in my room I thought I could hear laughter from the kitchen. He must have said something really dumb and she is laughing at him, I thought. When I finally came out and we got ready to leave, I asked, "When would you like me home, Mom?"

Her response nearly dumbfounded me.

"Whenever you like," she said and kissed me on the cheek.

When we lost her, my mother was just fifty-three. Suddenly, I had no one to turn to for advice about the decisions and choices of life, no one with whom I could share the joys and frustrations of raising a child. After a while, however, I began to feel her presence as if she were standing just behind me whispering in my eat. "Be patient, little boys are like that. He will grow out of it."

Then, little, unexplained things started happening. We would drive up to a restaurant with a completely full parking lot and, just as we drove up, someone would pull out of a space right next to the door. Our bank account would get low and out of the blue would come an unexpected tax refund.

While my husband, Michael, was in the Marine Corps and the family was living in North Carolina, we took a weekend trip to Colonial Williamsburg. Our oldest son, Aaron, and the only grandchild my mother ever knew, had taken along his faithful Bunny. Once a gorgeous Steiff rabbit with glistening fur and bright eyes, Bunny had been drooled on, slept with, and rubbed to the point where only Aaron could have loved him. And love him he did, for he would not travel, sleep, or eat without Bunny.

On the drive home from Williamsburg, we noticed that Bunny was missing. We stopped and called the restaurant that we had just been to and the motel where we had stayed the night before. Bunny was not to be found.

Aaron was beside himself. Suggestions of a new Bunny were met with tears. After two miserable days at home with this forlorn child, in frustration, I said to myself, *Where is my mother when I need her? She would know what to do.*

The moment I said this, the doorbell rang and there at our doorstep was a deliveryman with a package from the Holiday Inn where we had stayed. Inside, of course, was Bunny (whom we still have).

In the summer of 1996 our youngest son, Adam, was on his way to Europe. The trip was a high school graduation present, and he could not wait to go. His travel plan was to fly from Los Angeles to St. Louis and from there to London.

When he arrived in St. Louis, the people at TWA told him that his London flight had been canceled. Not to worry, they told him, they would fly him to New York, put him up for the night, and they would guarantee him a seat on a flight to Paris the following day.

Adam has inherited his grandmother's persistence; he pressed the gate attendants for a seat on a London flight that was leaving within the hour, which was now completely overbooked because of the flight cancellation. At the last minute, a seat opened up and Adam was on his way to London.

My husband, who was at the University of Virginia for the summer, woke me up the next morning with a phone call. "Have you heard from Adam? Do you know what TWA flight he was on?"

When I told him Adam had called me just after arriving in London, he told me to turn on CNN. There it was— TWA Flight 800 to Paris had exploded off the coast of Long Island, killing all 230 people aboard—the flight a less persistent eighteen-year-old might have been on.

I still miss my mother desperately. To this day, I agonize over the fact that four wonderful grandchildren never had the chance to see and know her. I have become convinced, however, that Mother has simply stepped into a new role: watching over me and those I love.

BIRTHDAY BROWNIES

Alexis Gonyeau

Alexis Gonyeau, fifty-four, is a retired orthopedic nurse. She feels that nurses are particularly attuned to opening their hearts to receive spiritual gifts. "It is a grace," she says. Originally from New England, Alexis now lives in the Southwest, where, in her spare time, she plays a lot of golf.

In mid-April of 1991 our family had come to grips with the fact that Mom was actively dying of metastatic stomach cancer. She had discontinued her chemotherapy ("the chemo will kill me before the cancer will") and was managing at home, with my Dad and sister to help her.

I flew in for a week's visit, not knowing that it would be the last time I would see her. As sick as she was, she managed to bake a special treat for me, a favorite of mine, brownies.

During the course of my week's visit, Dad and I polished off the large pan of brownies with great relish. Before I left to return home, Mom also summoned up enough loving energy to bake some brownies for me to take back to my husband and daughter. She knew how much they loved her cooking.

Mom died July 1 that same year. I flew back East to attend the funeral and to assist my Dad in cleaning up the house, which had become a hospice of sorts.

My birthday is July 13 and that year I celebrated it there with my family. My cousin and I went out for dinner on the eve of my birthday, and upon arriving home, my dad and I waited up until 12:20 A.M., the time I was born, to "officially" bring my birthday in.

As I fell asleep that night, I made a request. "Mom, it's my birthday. While we have been brought up to believe a certain way, here I am wondering if you are in a safe and comfortable place, and not in pain any more. If this is so, could you please give me a sign?"

I awoke about six-thirty in the morning. As I lay in bed I smelled brownies baking in the oven downstairs. I thought my sister had gotten up to make my favorite dessert for me on my special day.

I walked quietly downstairs, but no one was up yet. I thought, How strange!

Only when I walked back upstairs and into my bedroom and smelled the baking brownies once again, did I realize I had indeed received a special gift from my mom.

ELIZABETH

Rosemary Altea

 Rosemary Altea is a medium who works with a spirit guide named Grey Eagle. While many spirits are able to make contact easily through a medium, there are others who struggle for one reason or another. The following story is such an example. This excerpt is from Rosemary Altea's book, *The Eagle and the Rose*.

It was 1982. I was on my own and struggling to survive. I had been left with no money, enormous debts totaling thousands of pounds, and a house I couldn't afford to run.

Cash was something I needed desperately at this time, and although it would be nice to think that spiritual wealth is the only important thing in life, unfortunately this just isn't so.

We live in a material world in which we all have to earn money, one way or another, to pay our bills, to feed and clothe us and our families.

Mick knew this, and so he arranged for a group of people to meet, ten in all, for what he called a "clairvoyant party."

He didn't tell me about it until all the arrangements had been made, and at first I was angry and refused to do it. But when he mentioned that I would be paid a small fee . . . well, I was sunk. I needed the money.

Mick had known what a desperate state my finances

were in, and this was his way of putting a little cash in my pocket.

The "party" was held one evening in the home of Elizabeth. I was nervous and on edge. I didn't like the idea of working this way, able to give only fifteen minutes of my time to each person.

Mick had come with me and suggested that we all join together in prayer before I began. We joined hands, and as Mick prayed, everyone bowed heads—well, everyone but me, that is. I took the opportunity to study my potential clients.

But as I watched, I had a vision: Garland upon garland of tiny rosebuds began to appear all around the room, strung along the walls in long loops. They decorated the room in the most beautiful way, and they were a gorgeous shade of pink.

It was by no means the first time that Grey Eagle had given me strength and encouragement in this way. In fact, I remember one time I was very unhappy about a patient of mine, Margery, who had died of cancer. I could not help wishing that I had done more for her, although what more I could have done I did not know. As I was pondering on this one day, I became aware of a bright light shining out to the left of me, and as I looked toward it I saw the prettiest sight: masses of pansies, such lovely flowers, the markings on the petals looking so much like faces. They all seemed to be smiling at me as they waved in the breeze. As soon as I saw them I was reassured and smiled, knowing instantly that this vision was given to me by my guide so that I would know Margery was safe and happy, for you see, pansies were her favorite flower.

So it was, as in a vision, I saw those tiny pink rosebuds in such a spectacle of color that I felt a reassurance and immediately became less nervous. What a lovely way Grey

Eagle had chosen to let me know that he was with me! It never occurred to me that there might be another reason for the gift of flowers.

Despite my apprehension and misgivings about the evening, everything went well. I sat in the dining room, and one by one the ladies came to me for their sittings. For every one of them, evidence of survival after death was overwhelming.

It is always a pleasure for me to make communication links such as these. Over and over again I listen to the evidence from those in the spirit world, not only of their survival after death, but of their constant and continuing interest in the people they have left behind. Help and advice is given on so many subjects, even the most trivial—advice that is always valuable, whether it has to do with business, health, children, education, or affairs of the heart; advice made even more precious because it comes from those in the spirit world, who see so much more clearly than we, who are so easily blinded by emotions.

It is also possible for those in the spirit world to see farther ahead than we can, and so they are able to give help and advice concerning the future. And part of my pleasure comes from being able to help set people on the right track, of watching as enlightenment dawns with the knowledge that not one of us is alone and without aid of one kind or another. Even when the outlook for the future is not so good, those in the spirit world are able to give good and sound advice that will often ease a situation, giving strength and hope that the bad times will not last forever.

The last of my sittings that evening was with the hostess, Elizabeth. I had sensed how nervous she was immediately, so without delay I began.

Already I had begun to listen to Grey Eagle and, as

always, he told me all the things about her that I needed to know. As with all of my sittings, my first communication is with Grey Eagle, but I had still not looked at her as I said, "Now then, what's all this nonsense about rats?" And as I sat down in front of her, I looked into the most startled pair of blue eyes I had ever seen.

Continuing, I repeated, "Rats, you have been having dreadful nightmares about rats, haven't you?"

Speechless, she nodded, and huge tears bubbled up in her eyes and ran down her face.

I reached out and gently patted her hand. "Well, shall we see if I can help you?"

Nodding again, she whispered, "But how do you know, how could you possibly know about my dreams?"

"A medium is someone who quite simply is able to talk to the dead," I explained. "And I know about your dreams because my spirit guide, Grey Eagle, has been talking to me about you since you first walked into the room." I smiled a reassurance and then said, "Now, shall we continue and try to see if we can find out what this is about?" And, of course, we did just that—and we addressed her phobia.

A few days later I heard from Elizabeth again, and we arranged a time for her to see me.

"I'd like a proper sitting," she said. "Last time, your guide spoke to me. Now I would like to get in touch with my mother. I really need to know if she is all right and, of course, whether or not she really survived death."

"There are no guarantees that I can make contact with your mother, or that she will want to speak to me," I said. "I can only guarantee that I will try. The rest is up to her."

This agreed, Elizabeth came for her first "proper" consultation, but although I did have several communicators, I didn't manage to link at all with Elizabeth's mother.

Disappointed but determined to try again, Elizabeth made another booking.

Three sittings later, four attempts and four disappointments, and still I could not seem to form a link with the one person Elizabeth felt she needed to hear from.

"It's no good," I sighed after the fourth time, not liking to admit defeat myself. "I'm afraid I just cannot seem to find the right wavelength. Perhaps it would be better if you found another medium. Your mother might find it easier to communicate through someone else."

In tears she shook her head and tried to reassure me that it didn't matter. I suppose she was trying to convince herself as well.

I made us both a cup of tea, and we sat in silence for a while. Then, in an effort to cheer her up, I said, "Come on, it's not the end of the world, you know. How's Katie? Tell me how she's getting on." Katie was Elizabeth's handicapped daughter.

Immediately her face brightened and she began chattering away, telling me how her daughter had just been found a place at a special school and how well she was doing.

Nodding and sipping my tea, I listened as my friend chattered on. Then suddenly, I became aware of another lady also nodding and smiling as she listened to Elizabeth, standing quietly by her chair.

Not only did I see her clearly, I also heard her quite plainly as she turned her attention to me. "Hello," she said, "my name is Doris Rose. I'm Elizabeth's mother. I've been trying to get through to you for ages."

Without thinking, and cutting straight across what Elizabeth was now saying, I repeated what I had just heard.

The cup of tea that Elizabeth had been holding went sailing into the air, and a look of joy spread over her face. Bobbing her head up and down, she gasped, "It is, it is, that's my mother's name! Rose is my maiden name, Elizabeth Rose, and my mother is Doris Rose."

Doris Rose told us many things that day and was able to provide her daughter with the much needed evidence of her survival after death. She told of her illness, her cancer, and her struggle to fight it, how she thought she had succeeded until the day she became ill again and died shortly after. Describing that moment of death, Doris explained to me that her daughter had been sitting by her bed, holding her hand, and that the last thing Elizabeth did for her while she was alive was to wipe her face and dry her tears.

When I asked why it had taken so long, so many attempts on my part, to get through to her, she explained that she had been too nervous.

"Every time I tried," she said, "I just got the collywobbles, and couldn't do it. I hope you'll forgive me and understand." And of course, I did.

Then Doris went on to tell me how she had tried to let her daughter know that she was there on my first meeting with her.

"As you now know, my surname is Rose, and my favorite flowers are roses, and Elizabeth knows that more than any others, the tiny pink rosebuds, like the ones you first saw when you went to her house, are the ones I love the most.

"Grey Eagle placed garlands of them around the room for me, and I was hoping you would tell her about them, but you didn't."

The garlands of roses I had seen when I first went to Elizabeth's house. Oh, such a beautiful sight—but I had missed the significance of them. Such a small point, seemingly inconsequential. But because I hadn't seen it, I had failed to see Doris Rose.

Thank goodness that Doris and her daughter had persevered. Thank goodness they had kept on trying.

"If you had told her, I'm sure that my daughter would have realized the significance and known that I was there," Doris said then. "Perhaps," she concluded with a smile, "you could tell her that I will always be with her when she needs me, always."

A SKEPTIC CHECKS IN

Ethel Paquin

Originally from New England, Ethel Paquin began her writing career as a newspaper columnist and has published many novels, short stories, and articles. She is currently involved in writing the biography of the classical pianist Johana Harris, which is due for publication this year.

I am not a person who ever had easy contact with other dimensions—a little ESP, a couple of times of foreshadowing, that was about the size of it. I didn't dream about people who had died; I didn't get messages from them; I didn't have a strong feeling of their presence in my life.

I always envied people who could access friends and family who no longer lived in this world. I wished such contact were true, longed to see ghosts, but I never did. And I was envious, but at the same time a little skeptical, of those who said they did. After all, if they did and I didn't, it meant either they were imagining things, or for some reason or other my dearly departed didn't think me important enough to stay in contact with.

Sinclair told me often about the strong connection she had with her mother, dead now a number of years. Her mother left physical signs of her presence in my friend's life. When she asked me if I ever heard from my mother, I said I didn't. I told her my mother and I had not had the best of relationships. I said I wished there was some way for me to contact her and ask her what had been wrong between us, since I always felt that we had failed each other.

Sinclair asked if I had ever told my mother, straight-out, that I wanted to hear from her.

I hadn't. It had never occurred to me that was a step in the process. I always assumed the choice to get in touch or not to get in touch belonged to the person who had passed on. And I took it as another sign of my mother's lack of affection for me that she had never seemed the least interested in reaching out to me.

"You're wrong. Looking at you, no one would ever think you were missing that kind of connection," my friend said. "Maybe your mother doesn't know it either. Have you ever straight-out asked her for a sign that she's still with you?"

Well, no, I hadn't.

"I mean, they just don't hang around looking for the right time to get in touch, they have things to do too. You have to get their attention. Tell your mother, tell her out loud and often," she suggested. "Even if you think your relationship with her was lousy, it doesn't matter. The connection between a mother and a child is the strongest one there is. We all have problems that we deal with here in this life; maybe she was so involved with her problems she was overwhelmed, and it seemed to you as if she was uncaring."

That was possible. She certainly had a lot of problems to face, some of which I hadn't thought she'd handled all that well. And I can remember making that pretty clear to her.

"Nothing is stronger than the mother-child tie. Ask her!"

So without telling anyone what I was doing, I did ask. I asked out loud, often, and occasionally none too politely.

Now I need to tell you about my name. I was named for my mother, whose name was Ethel, and my middle name came from my grandmother, whose name was Carmina. It was a bulky, awkward package for a kid to labor under. I would rather have been named Mary or Elizabeth or Jane, anything but Ethel.

I hated my name. And in all of my school years I met only one other Ethel, and she hated her name too. In all of my life I doubt I've met more than three other Ethels.

My grandparents were Italian and there is no "th" in the Italian language, so they pronounced my name Ettel, which degenerated into Ettie, which became my family name.

A short time after my voiced requests to my mother for some sign that she was still with me, I was buying underwear. When I handed the salesgirl my charge card, she smiled at me and said, "My name's Ethel too." A week or two after that, I was visiting a friend who had a maiden aunt staying with her. I've known that friend for thirty years. The maiden aunt's name was Ethel. In all the years of our friendship she had never commented on the fact that her aunt and I had the same name. I began running into Ethels every time I turned around. The telemarketer who called was named Ethel. The woman who came to clean my house was named Ethel. Someone I was teamed up with to make a foursome for golf was named Ethel. A woman in a class I was taking was named Ethel.

And then, just before Christmas, I was looking for books as possible gifts and I came across a rather offbeat book about fairies, *Lady Cottington's Pressed Fairy Journal*, just the kind of book my mother would have loved. A line of the book read, "Nana wouldn't believe me, Ettie wouldn't believe me, Aunt Mercy wouldn't believe me, but I got one . . . I showed my fairy to Ettie, but she said Nana would be cross because my book is for pressing flowers in, not fairies."

I gave up. Not only was I sure it was my mother heeding my request, I knew she was doing it with my name purposely, giving me an elbow in the ribs. I had to laugh. I had forgotten that my mother had a great sense of humor.

So what was the gift my mother gave me? It's hard to explain in ten words or less. For one thing, she absolved me of the guilt I felt that my attitude was responsible for our strained relationship. It may have been part of the problem, but she doesn't hold it against me. I've lost the sorrow I used to drag around with me over the fact that my mother and I hadn't had the time to somehow get it together.

I know now we have all the time in the world. Her presence back in my life has done away with a lot of anger I don't think I knew I had. She's given me a feeling of support, the assurance that I'm not alone. I talk to her a lot these days. Probably more than I did in the two years before her death. I laugh with her a lot.

The problem now is that I miss her physical presence more than ever, but it's a good kind of missing. Not the missing I endured before she got in touch. Then I was filled with remorse that somehow we had never been able to understand one another. I felt that she was not all that interested in me and my needs. I know now that's not true, because the method she chose to contact me was so personal, so intimate, that no one who was not acutely aware of me as a person could have chosen it.

And, of course, I've been gifted with her spiritual presence, which will last for my lifetime and beyond.

LOVE BLOSSOMS

Kathy Alexander

Kathy Alexander, fifty-one, is a vice president and director of the Southern Arizona campus of the University of Phoenix.

As soon as Daddy called and told me about the cactus sending out the most amazing blossom he had ever seen, I knew it was from my mother. She should have heard him. He went on and on about how beautiful the flower was. He told me he took pictures of it and was sending copies to me. When he finally took a breath, I said to him, "Don't you think it's unusual that the cactus, which has been around for so many years, bloomed for the first time on Mother's birthday just a few weeks after she died?"

He didn't ponder this or think it unusual as I did. I hadn't told him about the agreement I had had with my mother that she would send a sign to me from the "hereafter." After all, she knew what he thought about this kind of talk.

My mother's deciding to use a flower as a symbol that she was thinking of me was such a perfect idea. Now I wonder if every flower that blooms is blessed by someone who has gone before.

My husband, Paul, paid my mother the greatest compliment. He said that she really knew how to die, and I agree with him. People seemed more and more drawn to her the closer she got to death. It was as if my mother possessed perfect clarity and could advise friends and family about their lives. And they felt as if they could truly believe what she told them.

When Mother was in the hospital, she told me that she would always be with me. At the time, I hoped she meant by those words that, in some way, I would see her or hear her or feel her presence as I always had, even after she was gone. But that didn't happen and, at first, I was a little disappointed.

As time goes by, however, I am beginning to realize that she is here with me in a way she understands, but I did not. Now, as never before, she is with me as my intuition, as my guide. My mother is with me every day. I think of her more often now than I did when she was alive, maybe because we are closer now—she is at the core of who and what I am.

Don't get me wrong. I would give so, so much to see my mother again, to be near her, and to have a chance for one of our talks. But I feel her close to me now, as she said I would.

I thank my mother for the beautiful cactus blossom and for all the help she sends to me daily.

I love her so much.

MARION'S JOURNEY TO HEAVEN

Barbara Ziehler

Barbara Ziehler, sixty, is retired from the marketing end of the insurance business. Disabled with Epstein-Barr virus, she breeds and shows horses, including a two-time world champion palomino quarter horse.

My mother, Marion, was a child prodigy. While she had had no formal training, she easily played seven to eight musical instruments. After graduation as the salutatorian of her high school, she went on to distinguish herself in college, eventually obtaining her master's degree.

My mother knew that life was to be lived. Death, however, was a different story. It was very frightening to her.

When she first became ill with the dreaded Alzheimer's disease, she tried very hard to keep things together. But of course, this was to no avail.

In the final two to three years of her life, she was desperate to be "whole" again and would repeatedly say, "O dear God, please help me, please help."

I, in turn, would say, "Are you ready to go live with your Father in heaven?"

A resounding "Hell no!" would come from her spunky Irish mouth.

Alzheimer's is an awful disease for everyone, so there is no use lamenting that. Marion, through it all, kept her sharp tongue and hilarious sense of humor until she lost

most of her ability to speak. She knew what she was saying but her audible sounds were gibberish to us.

The last four days of her life were tragic (did I give her
enough moisture?), revealing (the tiny body lying there is
how I came into this world), and historic in that it was the
end of an era (my mother—our good times, great times,
her ability to delegate, her humor, her teachings, her pride
in us, and of course, her deep love for us, her children).

At the end she could not speak and had not spoken for
many, many months—perhaps even a year or so.

Four days before she died there was a definite change
in her. She was alert and connected to someone or something outside of our sphere, but inside her room.

I stayed with my mother most of the time during her
last days, and I was amazed that she didn't pass sooner.
And then I realized why. Marion was communicating with
the spirit world, and I can only guess who they were. I'm
sure her dead twin sister was there. They were very close
in living life, and I'm sure Merle was trying to convince
my mother that it was OK to come over.

Although Marion did not speak, she communicated
with her angels for probably eight hours. She never moved
her eyes or head as she stared at a corner of her hospital
room.

I knew "they" were there. And I also knew she was
communicating and that the spirits were having trouble
convincing her it was wonderful and that they were there
waiting for her.

Suddenly she turned to me, looked right in my eyes,
and asked out loud, "Can you see them?"

I was so stunned that she could actually speak and
move, that regretfully I didn't ask her who was there. I
only said, "No, Mom, I can't see them but I know you can.
Are you ready to go with them and your heavenly Father?"

So typically Marion, she said, "Maybe." The angels at

least had been somewhat convincing, for this time she didn't say, "Hell no!"

After that, her attention returned to that spiritual corner, not to those of us who were with her in the physical room.

My sister, Madelyn, and her husband arrived the next evening, and we spent most of the next couple of days holding our mother, touching her, and trying to persuade her and ourselves that it was time to let go.

On Marion's last day she couldn't speak, but she would move her frail little body from one side of the bed to the other and grasp my hand and Madelyn's and, without speaking a word, she told us how much she loved us and how she would miss us greatly. Her hands remained strong and her message came through clearly.

At about 10 P.M. my husband convinced my sister, brother-in-law, and me to go have something to eat. That was his way of making us feel better—a very caring person coming to our rescue. I'll never forget saying to Mom, "We're going to go get something to eat and then we'll come back."

The minute that came out of my mouth, I couldn't believe I'd said it, for my mother had eaten nothing but ice for days, and I knew that she would never eat again. We mortals—how selfish we are! Ultimately I had to laugh at myself.

Our dinner was somewhat hurried but, in a way, calming. On our return to her bedside there was a definite change in the process, but Mother was still alive and breathing. We told her we loved her and wished her a good night and Godspeed.

The fifteen-minute drive home was somber and upon our arrival we immediately went to bed, my husband and I upstairs, my sister downstairs in the guest room.

The phone rang ten minutes later—Mother had died.

We wanted to see her once more, so we quickly dressed and returned to the hospital.

The minute we walked into the room (remember, only thirty to forty-five minutes had passed since we had left it), I realized that the angels were gone and there was no soul left in Marion. The physical body was empty. After a quick kiss on her forehead, we left.

Some time later, back in our respective beds at my house, we immediately fell asleep.

Suddenly I had one of the most terrifying experiences of my life. In 3-D motion, coming faster than I could ever imagine, were hundreds of ghastly faces coming toward me. With their intensity, for an instant I thought I was going insane. Then several angels appeared and one man touched my feet and held them with his hands and said, "It's okay. She'll be fine."

With that, the faces disappeared and I felt calm. The man who talked to me seemed familiar, but I didn't recognize him. I've come to realize that it was probably my brother who was born four years before me and who had died as a three-month-old infant.

The angels stopped in my sister's room that same night, but were much calmer. She had the feeling of them being there and then moving quickly on and was not as frightened as I was. We shared our experience the next morning without knowing that we were telling a similar story.

In the years since my mother's death, I call on her often.

She was raised in Utah on a dairy farm with horses and cattle. Not wanting to participate in any of that, she put that duty off on her twin sister so she could play her music.

Now when I travel with my horses, I ask my mother to go with me. I apologize for asking, because this is not what she would choose to do. But I need her with me and she comes.

When I'm driving in the truck to horse shows, she appears on my left side over the back of my shoulder and lets me know that she is there and that she will help me travel safely. And of course, the irony is that horses and country people are what she wanted to get away from most as a child.

The process of my mother's passing was an experience, to say the least. I'll never be the same again.

Thank goodness her last day on earth was not, and will not be, our last communication.

THE BIRTHDAY GIFT

Deb Whalen

⟳ Deb Whalen, forty-seven, has worked at many jobs—managing a contact lens lab, bartending, and working in physical therapy. Ten years ago, although she was broke, she decided to go back to school to pursue her dream. Today, Deb is a professional photographer.

It is early Friday afternoon. Yippee! I arrive home from work after lunch. It's my birthday this weekend and we are taking a trip to northern Arizona to stay in a cabin near Flagstaff. I pull into the driveway, going through my mental list of everything we need to take with us. We always take enough for a year, but what the heck. Maybe we'll luck out and get snowed in!

Hmmm, I'm thinking. Better soak the flowers out front really well before we leave. The scarlet poppies are getting ready to burst open, and one lone orange California poppy has already bloomed. The still-green hollyhocks are monsters, taller than me! The penstemon have already sent out their long stalks with tiny coral and pink trumpetlike blooms.

I fasten the showerlike sprinkler head onto the end of the hose, turn the water on low, and prop it on the ground for a gentle spray. As I round the corner of the sidewalk to admire the penstemon, I notice a movement by the flower stalks.

Butterfly, I think, as I turn my head to look. How lucky I am to see the first of the season.

To my delight, however, a busy little hummingbird, fearlessly close, startles me.

Wow, this is even better than a butterfly! I hold perfectly still while she methodically works around and around the little pink penstemon trumpet flowers. Hungry for nectar, she seems to take no notice of me, having more important things to tend to.

My partner, Janet, pulls into the driveway just then. "Shhh," I caution. "Look, a hummingbird." Janet looks in awe and appreciation from the driveway, watching for a few minutes, then hurries into the house. She can take advantage of my playing around in the front yard and get some presents wrapped.

After Janet's departure, the little bird then buzzes right over in front of me, to work on the coral flowers. She can't be more than a foot away from me.

Suddenly Mom comes to mind. My, how she loved hummingbirds. Seems like everyone in the family would bring her anything that had to do with hummingbird art. Oh, how I wish she could be here to see this.

It's hard to believe that it will soon be a year since she left this world. At the funeral home last year I tucked a little hummingbird magnet that had been on her fridge into her jacket pocket so she wouldn't be without her beloved bird.

My eyes cloud over and sting from the tears that suddenly well up. For some reason a well-loved children's book—called *Are You My Mother?*—comes to mind. I then start to chuckle and speak aloud to the tiny bird in front of me. "'Are you my mother? . . . I am not your mother,'" I quote from the book, "'I'm a steam shovel!'"

The little bird then zooms over to the gentle spray of water, takes a few quick dips, and zips over to the mesquite tree nearby. I don't know why, but I pursue the issue. "Will you come closer to me?" I whisper.

I think about how the little critter seems to like the water. Remembering a previous experience a couple of years ago when a hummer dipped herself in the hose spray as I watered, I slowly go over to the spray I had set up, and hold it up.

Zoom! Suddenly she is right in front of me, happily dipping her butt in the water, her little legs paddling. This time she is *inches* away from my fingers. She tries to land on the showerhead, but the water keeps pushing her back. I can barely contain my joy! She happily showers for several minutes.

She has a fluorescent green back, is whitish on her belly, and has a chin with little brown "freckles." What I really notice, though, is a bright red spot smack in the middle, under her chin. Hmmm, looks like a little necklace.

Happy with her bath, she zips back to the tree. As I watch her fluff her feathers from a distance, I notice that she has "stuff" all over her beak. Nectar or pollen, I think. I am truly feeling the presence of Mom. How she loved to eat heartily, often with crumbs or sauce on her chin, usually dropping some on the front of her blouse.

I watch in awe as the teeny bird preens and fluffs with her long, slender beak, carefully cleaning and drying herself. One more test, I think. "Will you touch me?" I say aloud reverently.

After watching her a bit longer, I advance slowly and without hesitation toward the tree and the tiny branch she is perched on. She never budges, continuing to clean. I stretch out my hand in front of me, palm down, little finger toward her.

As I get closer and closer, I never feel that she will leave. I level my hand right next to the branch she is on, forgetting to breathe. She steps on my little finger, touches my pinky ring with her beak, then gently lifts herself straight up with her tiny wings and sets herself back down on the branch right next to my hand!

I exhale slow and long. I am speechless. "Thank you," is all I can mutter as tears fill my eyes. "This is the *best* birthday present ever."

I continue to watch her for what seems like forever. She lifts up and transfers from branch to branch, never straying too far. After what seems like a good rest for her, she eventually busies herself with the flowers again. Just like Mom. "Hark!" she would say. "Let's get to it. We've got work to do."

The hummingbird with the little red necklace seems to go back to her duties, and so must I. Besides, I have to run inside and tell Janet.

A year earlier my mother couldn't speak or swallow due to her Lou Gehrig's disease. She wrote me a note saying she had missed my birthday and couldn't get me a card. She was very ill during my birthday time and obviously couldn't do much about it, directing my brother to write me a check for my "belated bday." So it was very significant that this year she chose my birthday to come to visit me.

Thank you, Mom, for the most precious birthday gift. I know you are happy and you are fine. When I start to miss you, I remember the little hummingbird you sent. I once again feel your presence, and cannot help but feel overwhelming joy.

MOMMA KNEW

Nola Ramsey

⌇⌇⌇ Nola Ramsey is a retired greenhouse manager. She
and her husband live in the mountains outside of
Grants, New Mexico, near Mount Taylor.

I'm the baby of my family, and my mother and I were extremely close. I lived with her until I was eighteen, and
she also lived with me on and off over the years. She
passed away ten years ago and her leaving was the hardest
thing I've ever gone through.

I was totally depressed after my mother's death. It took
years for me to get over her dying. I don't even know how
long, although my husband, Harry, could probably tell you
to the day.

When she died, the world changed. Everything was different, not necessarily uglier or worse, just different.

The hardest thing for me was to not have her for my
birthday. The rest of the holidays were bad, but my birthday was the worst. Once, when I was going through some
of her boxes and papers (my mother saved everything), I
found a birthday card that said "To Daughter." It wasn't
signed but I knew that it was meant for me, because I collect rabbits and there was a rabbit on it. I also knew that it
was meant for my next birthday.

She's with me always and I talk to her out loud all the
time and ask her questions. In this way, I try to keep her
with me as much as possible. I feel my mother's presence
a lot, and my husband does too. She was truly a good per-

son. I knew that then but I probably didn't tell her like I should have.

In retrospect, I should have asked my mother a lot more questions than I did. She was always there for me and I never took advantage of it. For instance, I don't have a history because I always thought that I'd just call Momma. No one knows your history better than your mother. Mine was with me through a lot in thirty-six years. She knew things I didn't know, things I wished she hadn't known, and things I forgot (or tried to). And she always loved me, no matter what.

My mother, like my husband and me, was a plant person. We had a joya plant that we started from cuttings from a plant Momma had. It's kind of a weird plant. It doesn't bloom very often. In fact, some say it has to be twenty-five years old to flower. After my mother passed away, I brought her plants to my house.

A year after her death, one of her plants started blooming. This was very close to her birthday, which was February 24. I told Harry that I would give almost anything if I could tell my mother that her plant was blooming.

"Well, she probably knows," he said. We're metaphysicians, so we think this way anyway.

I didn't think too much more about it.

I'd brought all of her belongings to my house, and I hadn't started going through them because I just couldn't bring myself to do it. They were downstairs near the laundry room. A short time later I was doing the laundry and I decided that I should just deal with it and I started going through her things. I was looking through a drawer with my mother's paperwork in it when I found a small blue business card from an optometrist where I used to work. I wondered why it was in her stuff, since it had been years since I'd worked there.

I turned the card over and it said, in her handwriting, "Noni, joya blooming."

I showed it to my husband when he got home and he said, "See, I told you Momma knew."

A QUIET SPACE

Jeanette Porter

Jeanette Porter spent seventeen years in the criminal justice system as a probation officer before staying home and raising her children. She is forty-two, has a black belt in tae kwan do, and is very active in the greyhound rescue effort, placing racing dogs in homes after their careers are over.

Although my mother and I only lived twenty minutes from each other, we talked on the phone every day without fail.

Mom died twelve years ago. A couple of days after her death, when I had gone back to work, I returned home to the blinking light of my answering machine. When I checked it, there was no message, no hang-up, just thirty seconds of blank tape.

This went on for two weeks. I'd come home from work to the flickering answering-machine light. There would be no messages or hang-ups. I'd rewind and every day the same amount of tape would be used.

When I finally mentioned what was happening to a friend of mine, I said, "I know this is her way of letting us know that she's OK, but it's kind of scaring me." After that there were no more blank messages.

She called my father too. He's in the carpet business and he was installing a carpet about a month after my mother's death. He was at a customer's house when the phone rang.

"It's for you," the man said, after listening to the woman on the other end ask for Ralph.

"Who is it?" my father asked since he had no idea who it could possibly be. My mother was always the one to set up his calls, and she was no longer there to do that for him. There was no one he knew who would have known that he was at that number, at that house.

"I don't know. It's a woman," the customer said, handing over the telephone.

When my father took the receiver, there was no one there.

DREAM WORK

Kathy Colletti

A professional dollmaker, Kathy Colletti was honored at the 1988 New York Toy Fair for her one-of-a-kind dolls. She is represented by several galleries in the Southwest.

I was adopted at birth and was never very close to my adoptive mother. She was one of eleven children from a large farming community in Indiana. I don't remember her ever forming close friendships with anyone except her sister.

My father was a carpenter and my mother was a full-time homemaker who never drove a car, flew in an airplane, or went anywhere except to Chicago several times to visit relatives.

Our family was a very closed system. Mother had arthritis and life was hard for her. She rested in a living room chair that she claimed as her own. The smells coming from that chair were of Camel cigarettes, Avon perfume, and Vicks VapoRub, which Mother thought was the cure for all of life's ills. We owned an industrial-size jar that sat on our kitchen table right next to her prayer books.

I had little memory of certain parts of my childhood. I was always getting into trouble, did poorly in school, and had deep, explosive fits of anger. Unhappy, over the years I would go to my mother trying to get answers for the crazy feelings that led to my destructive behavior. Her response was always, "You just don't know what your father has done."

Shortly after I graduated from high school, I distanced myself from the family by moving 120 miles away to Tucson. My mother, who was almost fifty when she adopted me, deteriorated over the years with health problems. I traveled back and forth between Tucson and Phoenix on a regular basis.

At eighty, Mother was forced to go into a rest home. From there it was downhill.

I was thirty years old, divorced with two children, and dating a man who lived in Phoenix. I was still angry, had addictions that were out of control, and unexplained chronic health problems were beginning to surface.

Wanting desperately to stop hurting others and myself, I went into therapy. My therapist thought there were some pretty serious secrets locked behind the walls of anger I used as protection. I made a commitment to get the help I needed in order to heal.

The last time Mother was hospitalized, my brother Larry summoned me to Phoenix. Since it was very late when I arrived, I went straight to my boyfriend's house. I would see my mother first thing the next day.

At four-thirty in the morning I was slightly awakened by the strong aroma of Vicks VapoRub. I turned to the side of the bed and saw my mother standing there in her hospital gown. She was in solid form, surrounded by a misty cloud. She said in a very clear voice, "Kathy, promise me when you remember what happened in your childhood you won't write a book." When I told her I couldn't promise that, she disappeared.

The ringing telephone brought me fully awake. It was my brother calling to tell me Mom had just died. At the moment of her death she had given me one last confusing message—*Promise me when you remember what happened in your childhood you won't write a book.*

After her death I got really serious about my therapy. I

explored Jungian analysis, which concentrates on dream work.

New information was always preceded by a recurring dream. In it I was unable to see, yet I was still aware that the world was turned upside down. I was crawling to a telephone for help, but the phone wouldn't work, so I couldn't connect with anyone.

Every time I had the dream, bits and pieces of my missing childhood surfaced.

My breakthrough came the last time I ever had the familiar dream. I was still terrified that my vision would not clear, I was still disturbed by the upside-down world, and I still hated my desperate crawl to the dead telephone. But this time a large black woman who looked like Aunt Jemima told me to open my eyes and look at her. I did. And the woman held me, rocked me, and gave me the final pieces to my childhood puzzle.

My adoptive father had had a drinking problem. He flew into a rage when I was eleven and threw me into a metal pole that held up the sink in the bathroom. The occipital lobe at the base of my brain was hit, not only giving me a concussion, but also rendering large parts of my childhood irretrievable to me for almost thirty years.

At eleven, left to deal with the injury, the emotional trauma, and the confusion, I dealt with it the only way I knew how—I buried it.

After Aunt Jemima explained things to me, I never had the dream again.

Looking back, I know the black woman in the dream was my mother coming to me. We had a black, red, and white Aunt Jemima cookie jar that sat on our kitchen counter all the time I was growing up. That cookie jar held my mother's famous chocolate chip cookies. Baking was the most nurturing expression of love she had. She knew that the woman on the jar was the perfect symbol.

I believe that only through her death was my mother free to come to me and give me the gift of answers to my questions. She had so much shame, she couldn't face me when she was alive, Aunt Jemima was the symbol her spirit chose to communicate with me.

After that last dream I began to get my life and my health back.

THE TWENTY-SECOND OF EVERYTHING

Judith Marcovitch

Judith Marcovitch is the director of sponsorship sales for the event division of a leading women's publication. She has inherited her hobby from her mother, as she is passionate about, and addicted to, hunting for treasures in thrift shops, flea markets, and auctions. Over fifty, she lives in New York City.

On September 22, 1995, at 2:30 A.M., the phone rang.

"Judy," my father began, "I've got some bad news. Mommy is dead."

A bolt of lightning struck. It electrified me; never before was I so alert, yet so completely numb. As with John Kennedy's assassination, I remember not only where I was when I heard the news, I also recall those unspoiled innocent seconds before.

I remember the state of sleep, my position in bed, the room as it was before I reached over to turn on the light to reach the connection that would change my life forever . . . dividing it into Before Her Death and After Her Death.

Unaware that Mom had been feeling ill, I was totally unprepared for that early morning call. From the moment I lifted the receiver, another force, a different energy, took over. In the midst of the most extraordinary grief and pain I had ever felt, I had this incredible energy.

Mother had had a heart attack the previous December.

After this scare, the doctor said she was fine and assured us that while she had several other medical problems, including a rare blood disease, she would not die of a heart attack. Which, of course, is what killed her.

We all thought, including Mom, that when she did die it would be in a hospital with megadoses of medicine, tubes, breathing devices, and suffering, especially suffering. Two weeks before her death she had a dream that her mother had come for her. But she told her she wasn't ready, not just yet.

My mother and I had a nice relationship. My parents lived in Florida; I lived in New York. I was pleased with the distance. Before my mother's death, my daughter Bonnie and I went for a "women's weekend" with my mother and sister, Jaye. We toured South Beach, laughed a lot as we usually did when we were all together, and went to Sawgrass Mall to shop. In fact, the outfit Mom bought on that day, a to-die for Fendi jacket and a steal at only five hundred dollars, was the one she would wear to her funeral.

By the time I arrived in Florida, my father had already made the arrangements and called a consignment shop to arrange for a family friend who worked there to pick up her things.

As I went through my mother's clothes to decide what she was going to be cremated in, I had a strange sensation that we were doing this together. That she was not gone, but there with me, guiding me from one hanger, one drawer, to the next. It was as though we were together in this private place, in a protective, sunny bubble.

Because arrangements had already been made with the consignment shop, I knew that my sister and I had to go through all of Mother's things within the next few days. Again, there was no question in my mind as to what was to be done. Everything flowed in a symphony that seemed to be orchestrated by her. It was another world.

My mother was a handbag and jewelry designer and a true collector. Her passion was shopping in thrift stores, where she found discarded valuable antiques. She had two hundred pairs of shoes, hundreds of pocketbooks, collections of real and costume jewelry, and several closetfuls of clothes.

She also neatly categorized all of her business papers and receipts. She even saved 1970s auction catalogues from Sotheby's and Christie's.

Jaye and I needed to go through everything and peacefully decide what each of us wanted. This was the ultimate shopping excursion—a trip to our mother's closet.

We did shoes and jewelry one night, pocketbooks another, and the clothing we saved for last.

During the process, Jaye, a dishrag of uncontrollable sobs, began falling apart. It was then that I asked my mother for help. Out loud I said, "Mom, I can't do this alone; you've got to send Jaye a sign that this is what you want us to do."

My sister had to go to the bathroom, the same one we had used for fifteen years. Suddenly the ceiling fan went completely haywire and made a horrible screeching noise. Jaye was so startled that she shrieked and jumped off the toilet seat. She was impressed enough to continue cleaning out Mother's closet.

At the funeral, my sister and I walked into the chapel holding hands. I took the deepest breath as I prepared myself for the moment when I would actually see my mother dead. I was bracing myself for the end of the safe haven in which I had been sheltered for the past few days. Instead, as I looked at my mother for the last time, I experienced elation and, most strangely, a sense of gratitude. It was as though my mother was at peace and thanking me for taking care of her worldly possessions just as she had wanted.

For two years, on the twenty-second of each month or on my birthday I received a gift from my mother. I would find a duplicate of one of her finds when I was shopping, one of her favorite songs would be playing in the store, an important sale for my business would come through, or I'd have a small win on a lottery ticket; all were unexpected gifts.

On December 22, 1995, two months after she died, I found a letter that she had written to my father, my sister, and me requesting that she be allowed to die in her own home and trusting us to carry out her wishes. She did the former, and I like to feel we did the latter.

One twenty-second night I heard her whisper, "Judy," just "Judy" in my ear. It is impossible to describe the feeling of her breath against my skin and the warmth I felt shudder through me.

Even if I was unaware of the date, something would happen to remind me that it was the twenty-second.

On the twenty-second of April, 1996, I was riding on the New York subway and a magician appeared. He started to do tricks. The tourists beside me were enchanted, but he kept looking at me, smiling, and at the end handed me a piece of paper that read, "Do what you do best at your own pace in your own hand. Your lucky no. 22. Magic Lorenz."

Another month I had concert tickets to what I thought was a Kitaro concert. After being seated and seeing Seiji Ozawa of the Boston Symphony Orchestra come on stage and lead the orchestra in "Romeo and Juliet," my mother's and my favorite opera, I realized I had gone to Carnegie Hall *on the wrong night* and they sat me in the fifth row center anyway.

On September 22, 1998, I finally sold an antique Chinese screen and wedding headboard on eBay that had had no response before and that had also been turned down by a New York auction house.

The yearly anniversaries of my mother's death are especially significant. I go to thrift shops to see if she has left any messages for me. On the fourth anniversary of her death I went to one store I had not been to before. There in the showcase, under several other things on the bottom shelf, was a paper case that looked interesting. It turned out to be a 1950s limited edition book of tiny hand-painted Japanese prints and poems. The paintings were reproductions of seventeenth-century woodblock prints that my mother had bought at auction and dearly loved. I had just had them reframed and hung in my living room.

I still receive gifts that I now realize are really thank-yous. The more I think about it, I see that they come after I have unwittingly done something that she would have wanted me to do on her behalf.

And I, in turn, thank my mother for her wonderful gifts.

DON'T SELL YOURSELF SHORT

Mary Tate Engels

Mary Tate Engels is the author of twenty-nine novels and two nonfiction books. Her latest books include *Tales from Wide Ruins: Jean and Bill Cousins, Traders* and *Corazon Contento: Sonoran Recipes and Stories from the Heart*, cowritten with Madelaine Gallego Thorpe. Mary is the mother of three boys and lives with her husband in Tucson.

As my mother lay dying at home last summer in Tennessee, a poor, confused cardinal fluttered repeatedly against her bedroom window, trying to get inside. The daily struggle seemed especially unlikely because this was no clear, showy window that often lures birds. Hers was an ordinary frame house with small-paned, shadowed windows.

Day after day he floundered on the window beside her bed, drawing our attention and giving us a slight diversion. My mother would smile and speak to him. "Hey, sugar, you want to come in? My, my, aren't you beautiful?" The next day she would ask, "Where's my cardinal?"

On the day she died, he was gone. And I must admit, with my grief and dealing with her death, I forgot about the bird.

That winter, back at home in Tucson, I saw a brilliant cardinal and recalled the beauty and distraction that the Tennessee redbird had added to those bleak days. In the moment, memories of Mama came flooding back—how she loved nature, her lovely iris gardens, the pleasure she took during her last days in the beautiful cardinal who persisted in trying to get into her bedroom.

After experiencing her loss, I became particularly aware of making every day count and evaluating my own happiness. I was having a difficult time at work and missed being able to write. I could hear her Southern voice giving me advice: "Don't sell yourself short." Today we tell our kids, "Don't settle for less," "Actualize your potential," "Find your voice."

Part of my grieving for my mother was that she hadn't actualized her potential. She was a Southern woman; she was devoted to her husband and never made a decision without his sanction. After his death, she made almost no decisions, and the few she made for herself were poor and without good evaluation. After all, she had no practice for finding her own voice, although she encouraged me to do so. I felt that she had settled for less in the thirteen years since my father's death, so I grieved for the happiness she could have created for herself, but didn't.

Personally, I had been agonizing for months over a decision to quit my job, start my own business, and go back to writing. I made lists of pros and cons, evaluated it *ad nauseam*, and vacillated back and forth until even I was sick of talking about it. Still, the niggling desire to establish my own business wouldn't go away. Deep down, I wanted to do something more creative. And I realized that I was like my mother—stuck and unable to make a decision.

After yet another lengthy discussion, my husband helped me create a plan of action with an end date and pledged to support me, whatever my decision. *My decision.* I had to take a walk and think. I needed the clarity of open space, room to decide. I got no further than the end of my driveway when I saw an absolutely brilliant cardinal—and Mama's words came back to me, as clear as if she were standing right there. "Don't sell yourself short."

I hadn't seen a cardinal for ages. I thought they'd all gone back to Tennessee.

I knew in that moment that I'd been selling myself short in this job. I knew what I must do to find my voice, to create my own happiness. I felt my mother's presence, heard her voice. I knew she was there for me, giving me advice that she was never quite able to follow. "Don't sell yourself short."

Thank you, Mama. I'm listening.

THE RIGHT TICKET

Soma

～ Soma is an artist living in Tenaja, California. A mediator, she says she is here to care, to share, and to love.

In September 1994 the doctors at the nursing home in Washington, D.C., advised the family that my mother was ready to die "any day now." There was an art show there at the time, in a gallery founded by President Kennedy's sister Jean, featuring one of my paintings. Luckily I was able to travel not only for the opening of the show but also to say good-bye to my mother in her final days.

I went to see her, but although I was her favorite daughter, I'm not sure she even recognized me. She was ninety-four then and had lived a most remarkable life. Born into the aristocratic Song family during the reign of the last king of the Yi dynasty, she survived both the forty-year Japanese occupation of Korea and the Korean War.

After I returned home, my mother visited me in my dreams almost every night. One time she was wearing a long white robe with golden embroidery down the front. She stood very tall and did not speak.

One morning it dawned on me that she was telling me to prepare for her funeral by writing her eulogy. So I began. It took me weeks and weeks, interviewing family members here and in Korea, to assemble all of the history I needed to tell the story of her exceptional life.

On January 20, 1995, my pregnant niece was having a morning cup of tea at her home in California and glanced at the large sliding glass door. Outside the glass, looking in, was her grandmother—my mother—wearing a white dress. For a moment she thought she was really there, so she called out "Halmoni!" (which is the Korean word for grandmother) and then my mother vanished. My niece said she then realized that her grandmother was in Washington and that it was a very frightening experience.

The next day, my sister called me to tell me that Mother had died that day in Washington, D.C. We cried together long-distance. After my sister hung up, her daughter called her to report that grandmother had appeared again, that very morning, outside the glass door. So my sister told her that her grandmother had just died.

At the time, I could not afford another trip to Washington. My niece was unable to fly during her pregnancy, so she offered to buy my ticket to the funeral ceremony.

I believe that my mother appeared to my niece in order to facilitate my trip to the funeral and deliver the detailed, respectful eulogy I had taken so many weeks to prepare.

January 21 was also the day that Rose Kennedy died. President Kennedy was very popular in Korea, and his assassination was taken very hard. Knowing my mother, I suspect she chose that day to accompany Mrs. Kennedy.

At the funeral, I felt that my mother was watching everything and enjoying all the pomp and ceremony. I knew she was enjoying her freedom, shed of her tired old body.

Once again she was free.

MOM'S STICKY FINGERS

Rosemary Shearer

Rosemary Shearer has been active in politics, real estate, and the environmental movement for over thirty years. A founding member of the Superstition Area Land Trust (SALT) in Arizona, she enjoys reading, travel, movies, and needlework.

My mother's method of making herself known to me is less a gift than it is—well, there's no other way to put it—a prank, or a series of pranks.

Mom died quite suddenly in 1986, only four days before she, my husband, and I were to move to Arizona. For her it was a return to the desert she loved; for us it was a much anticipated new start, a move from our home state of Iowa to the same desert she and my father had introduced us to fifteen years earlier.

Mom believed in reincarnation and suspected that it also was possible to communicate after death. At age eighty-five, she had come to terms with her mortality, and we often carried on lively discussions about the mysteries of life and death.

Her sudden fatal heart attack was a terrible shock to our entire family. We knew her heart was frail, but she was such a vital, active woman despite her blindness, and was so excited about moving back to the desert, that it was unthinkable that she would leave just as she was about to begin anew.

Our house was sold, and the new owners were moving in at week's end, so our final preparations for Mom's funeral were launched with a heavy heart coupled with a sense of urgency. Many decisions were required, most of them painful, some foolish.

Under great stress, I arbitrarily decided not to keep some items I knew she wanted me to have: twelve place settings of sterling silver she had bought during the Depression by saving and rolling dimes for years, a beloved dining table and hutch from the Amana Colonies, and countless other items of less personal value were relegated to a storage shed to be later sold at auction. As I signed the papers, I vowed I'd never look back with regret for making these final decisions. Self-recrimination has reared its ugly head on several occasions, but I resist wallowing.

It was almost a year later, soon after we moved into our new house, that I began to wonder if she had "found" us. Things began to vanish.

We had built on family land next door to the home she and my father had lived in for years, on Kings Ranch in the Superstition Mountains southeast of Phoenix. I'm not a meticulous housekeeper by any stretch of the imagination, so my husband is careful to put important items in specific places. We used a hinged fireplace log handler for transplanting our prickly desert plants. Without it, this task was rife with discomfort, and it was an essential lawn tool. Large, black, and made of wrought iron, it was easily spotted in its usual place in the garage against a stark white wall.

I was working at the computer when my husband came in from the yard to ask me where it was. I had seen it the day before in its usual place, but he insisted, somewhat accusingly, that it was not where it belonged. We both searched the garage, then the grounds. We finally gave up and I returned to the house to finish my writing. A short while later, I glanced out the window to see him moving cactus with the implement. I asked him when he came in for lunch where he had found it.

"It was right where you put it," he said.

"What do you mean?"

"Come on, you found it and put it back where we always store it."

I laughed and told him I hadn't found it—that I'd come back in the house after our yard search. He looked at me very oddly and said, "But it was in the garage, right where we always keep it." He insisted that I was messing with him and wouldn't believe that I hadn't snuck it back to its proper place as a joke. We both agreed it was very strange, but he continued to believe I was toying with him.

It was several months later, near Christmas, and I had unpacked our ornaments and laid them out to begin decorating for the season. A pewter, hand-painted partridge, which I had bought during a trip with a dear friend who died of cancer shortly after our journey, held deep sentimental value. I carefully laid it on the mantelpiece to use in a display. I finished the rest of the room and went to retrieve the ornament, but it was gone.

I rummaged through the packing boxes, sorted through the trash, moved furniture, tossed couch cushions in search of the little partridge. I was near tears when I couldn't find it. I had cleared the mantelpiece of everything and couldn't think where to look next. Feeling sad, I went out to the yard to cut the evergreen boughs for the mantel display, and finished decorating without it.

Some time later, I was dusting the mantelpiece and there sat the little partridge—exactly where I had placed it smack in the middle of the mantelpiece, all by itself. I looked around, feeling rather foolish because I knew no one was home. I didn't feel anything or sense any presence, but I knew then that it was Mother, letting me know she was near.

On another occasion, one morning my husband's hearing aid was not in its usual spot on the dresser, and he had an important meeting. We rummaged drawers, searched under the bed, through the bed covers, frantically looking for it. Finally he had to leave and rushed out of the house, more than a little vexed at the inconvenience.

I went back to the bedroom to make the bed, shower, and get dressed. There, in plain sight, right where he was absolutely sure he had put it the night before, and where we both had searched several times, sat the hearing aid. This time I was onto her tricks, and after my goose bumps subsided, I said "Mom! Cut that out!"

There have been many vanishings and reappearances during the almost fifteen years since Mom left us. Sometimes I just laugh and say, "OK, Mom—very funny. Put it back!" Other times I become a bit annoyed, and ask out loud for her to please put it back, but I always let her know that I know she's here and how happy I am for her presence.

Mom was a gentle but firm disciplinarian. She believed in making the punishment fit the crime. When my brother ran away from home at age four, she tied him to the piano leg with a dishtowel for a half hour to teach him to stay put. (He went on to become a brilliant pianist, so apparently suffered few scars.) On more than one occasion, my mouth was washed out with soap for using language unseemly for a young lady. So I've often wondered, Is hiding important items from me her payback for my callous dispensing of her precious keepsakes?

I've recently come to terms with the idea that I was very, very angry at her leaving so soon, just when we were prepared to start a new life in her beloved Sonoran Desert. I've apologized to her and asked her forgiveness.

I can guarantee you, my housekeeping has not improved, nor as I grow older has my memory, but I've noticed of late that things have stopped vanishing and reappearing suddenly. She always returned my things, except for two keepsake rings that remain missing, but the sentimental belongings I disposed of are gone forever. Who knows? Once we finally sort out all this karma, my husband's and my old wedding rings may return.

THE MIRACLE OF DANDELIONS

Flynnie Meyer

Flynnie, a former family counselor, is an avid golfer and hiker. She is active in a mentoring program where she helps young children with their schoolwork.

Call it what you will. I call it a miracle. But when I need to feel my mother's love, dandelions appear.

They were there to greet me as I finished my morning run on the November day of my daughter's wedding. They were there for me, a beautiful group of them nestled next to a rock, to lighten my spirits as I hiked alone in Telluride on one of the darkest days of my life.

No matter how unlikely the time of year (even during Ohio winters!), they appear when I need a little boost, a little courage, a little strength like the kind you get from a mother's hug. There they are, those funny little flowers, poking their heads up at me, reminding me how as a little girl I once filled my tiny hands full of the yellow blossoms for my mother.

They appear to remind me how my mother would hug me tenderly for the gift, making me feel like no one else in the world had ever given her a more precious bouquet. She would arrange the blossoms with care in the finest cut-glass vase she could find in the house. And when the flowers wilted within the hour, I would be back at my task, gathering more for her.

Now these dandelions are there again when I need them, just like the love was there for me in my mother's eyes. I can't explain it. I just know it always happens, just like the sun rising. I call that a miracle, too.

BABY DOLL

Rowena Sinclair-Long

Rowena Sinclair-Long, forty-four, lives in a small town in rural Nevada. Married, with four children, she is a consultant/facilitator, a substitute teacher, and a soccer coach. Rowena also practices the arts of interior design, feng shui, and watercolor painting.

It seems the most successful times in my life are the times that my mother visits me. As I write this I begin to feel laughter, and, of course, tears. My mother was a fantastic woman who enlightened me, although I was too thickheaded and confident in her undying presence to realize it.

After my mother's death, the first time I really knew she was around was when I was heading to the hospital in Elko, Nevada, to give birth to my third child, Derek. Mother had been dead about four months, and I was fine, physically at least.

We were headed to the hospital seventy miles away and going through a construction zone and wondering if we'd make it in time.

As we got to a small town called Hunter, I was thinking that that would be a good name for the baby. Suddenly I started bawling because I missed my mother so much, but then I realized she really was with me. Maybe it had to do with the naming of Derek, because we had talked a lot about names for the baby before she died. And this baby had a special connection to my mom.

Right before she died, she was in the hospital. I was

pregnant with Derek. I drove 850 miles from Battle Mountain, Nevada, praying throughout the drive that my mother would still be coherent when I arrived.

My prayers were answered. I remember she was really, really weak, but she put her hand on my stomach and the baby kicked her. I said, "Momma, there's the baby." Her whole face lit up and it was so weird that he kicked right where her hand was, because she was so weak she never would have felt it anywhere else. That was a really cool thing. I think there's a real connection between unborn babies and dead people.

I felt robbed that she wasn't around and that she wouldn't be the one who would stay with me after I came home with the new baby. It was all really sad.

Looking back on that time, I remember being so worried that I'd have a dark-haired little girl who would look like my mother. Not even halfway through my pregnancy, I thought about the "look-alike" that could be inside of me. I was still in mourning and that would have been very difficult for me.

And what did I have? A blue-eyed blond little boy. I always felt that it was a blessing from God that Madison, my brown-haired little girl, came a year and a half later, since by then I was ready for that connection with my mother.

When Madison was almost one year old, Derek began calling her Mimi, not knowing of any connection with my mom. This was the name that all of my mother's grandchildren called her. Maybe it made sense because he was in that "before birth" place during and after my mom's death. When I think about it, it really was amazing that out of all the names he could have chosen for his little sister, he picked Mimi.

The older kids tried to dissuade him by saying, "Derek, Mimi is Mommy's mommy." But he would have none of it, insisting on calling his younger sister by my mother's grandmother name. To this day, Mimi is still Madison's nickname.

I guess I've never felt like my mother didn't know Madison and Derek. I know she knows them in another way. Sometimes the kids wake up crying because they've dreamed about her, and I feel in this way that they've spent time with her.

My mother has also made a connection with me in the way of white feathers. "Mimi feathers," as I like to call them, have been in my life since my mother died. My awareness of them was aroused after a conversation with my sister about the feathers she was receiving. She also mentioned an experience her artist friend had with white feathers. Lynn, the artist, always had a special connection to my mom with their love of art and my mom's love of theater and her drills of blowing feathers in the air to develop diaphragm strength.

Anyway, after my sister told me about the feathers, I began to pay attention. Sure enough, I was getting them from Mother too. It was always during times that I wasn't taking care of myself or running myself down with too many commitments.

One time I was very ill and couldn't move off the couch with two toddlers and two primary school children. Mother came to me and softly let a white feather fall to the floor to let me know that this too would pass.

Recently, while driving my now five-year-old Madison to school, she squealed with delight that she had found Mimi.

"Look, Mommy, Mimi's here! I found this feather!"

And, of course, as I looked at the feather, I knew she was right. It was one of *those* feathers that are "the Mimi feathers." I don't know how I know those feathers—there are not that many of them that she has shared with me over the years—but it was right, nonetheless.

This morning was typical, hectic and horrendous as usual, getting four children off to elementary school. Why was she supporting me now? Well, I needed her—it was that simple. Thanks, Ma.

Madison, who never knew my mother, frequently says, "I wish I'd known Mimi."

I say, "But you did know Mimi. I think you got to know Mimi in heaven."

And she says, "Yeah, I know." She says it with so much confidence.

A year and a half ago we bought six huge cottonwood trees to plant here on our property. I'm partial to cottonwoods because of an old farm we once had. My husband, Steve, had an opportunity to be in a golf tournament the Sunday after the trees arrived, and I said, "Go. I'll plant the trees."

The nursery man came out and dug the holes. These trees had four-inch trunks and big root balls, so my day was cut out for me. As I'm working in the yard, planting the trees, I'm thinking, *What a great legacy Mother has given us,* because we all love gardening. It's June and my hands have dirt on them.

I plopped in that first tree and packed it down and felt like a woman of the earth because I was planting these trees myself. Throughout the day, I thought of my mother and how neat it was that I was planting trees and she had loved to garden. It was almost like she was beside me that day, helping me plant the cottonwoods.

When I finally went to bed and thought about how I had been thinking of her all day long, it occurred to me that there must have been a reason. Then I noticed what day it was. June 1, the day she died, yet I hadn't thought of that once all day.

At every home I've ever lived in when my mother was living, she helped me plant—trees, wildflowers, vegetables, flowers. In fact, five weeks before she died we went to Target and she bought me a plant.

So there was that day, June 1, and although she had died, she was still with me. That's that ability to connect to that other world or whatever we want to call it. It's right there in front of our face, although we can't see it or smell it. We're just beginning to scratch the surface of understanding. Although this is probably a poor analogy, it's kind of like when computers were first introduced and wasn't it amazing that we could delete words and move them and move paragraphs? And now there's a place where you can call up your buddy on the Internet and you can have a visual and vocal conversation with that person. That's the kind of leap we're talking about now.

You know how they say when people die there is a realization that life here on earth is just a blink? Think of the effort that it must take to capture or tap into this blink of existence. It's amazing when your thoughts go a certain way and you just know that it's a conversation with your mom.

We do not know the life that is just outside our realm of reality or perspective. It's like intuition. There's no scientific explanation for intuition. The telephone rings and you know who it is. There's a spiritual ability, a spiritual connection that connects the world we know and the world we don't. It's unrecognized and undeveloped. They say that new babies and their mothers have telepathic ability, but then we keep verbalizing everything and that kind of communication is eventually diminished.

Not long ago I had been at work until the wee hours writing a grant application for youth-at-risk, infants to be exact. I came home, exhausted, and put on my "jammies" and collapsed on the sofa to read. Suddenly I heard a strange noise at the other end of the house. After investigating, I found a baby doll on its back on the dryer where I had left it to dry. Only now it was *crying*.

Why was it crying? It was one of those obnoxious dolls that cry when you push their stomach and stop when you squeeze their hand. I was very disturbed thinking that the exorcist was needed at my house *right now!* What was so amazing was that in order to make the obnoxious doll cry, a person really has to put a lot of pressure on her stomach to make her wail obsessively. Yet no one was touching her.

But after taking a deep breath (toxic gases had built up in my lungs for the last five minutes), I realized without question that Momma was giving me a message.

"OK, OK, I know I've been pushing myself too hard. Yeah, I know, I'll get some rest and take care of myself." Then I thought, "I sure miss you, Ma . . . thanks."

Maybe sometimes we just have to listen.

The next morning my sister called and told me she was collecting stories for this book.

Just a coincidence?

I don't think so.

RADIO WAVES

Nancy Fahringer

◠ Nancy Fahringer is a former classical radio disk jockey. Her hobbies include horseback riding and traveling.

I am an only child. My early memories are of my mother humming while she worked in the kitchen, sun streaming through the windows, and of her reading me *Ladies' Home Journal* nature columns by Gladys Taber. We had the most traditional of fifties East Coast lives, enjoying prosperity, hard-won and relished, as my parents were children of the Great Depression. My father never stopped marveling at what he'd gained by working six, sometimes seven days a week, celebrating by trips with us to Europe, by hiring a sculptor to do my mother and me, by buying a Connecticut country home on an island. "If I died tomorrow, I'd die a happy man," he'd say.

He did die early and suddenly, a stroke felling him at work. I had become married a month or so before his death, so within a short time my mother's life abruptly changed.

In the thirty years remaining to her, she, the reserved and dependent helpmate to my father, surprised us all by quadrupling the nest egg she'd been left and by traveling extensively—a cruise around the world, hummingbird watching in the Bahamas.

Despite a devastating auto crash in Arizona in which her car was broadsided, she didn't lose her enthusiasm for the West. After she recovered, she built a place in Tucson and, in her new home and garden, created the same security and beauty for my children that she had for me . . . even to the humming in the kitchen while she cooked, the bird-feeding, and her love of the outdoors.

Sadly, her last years were hellish—failing kidneys, round-the-clock nurses in her home. At the same time, I was beginning a 4:30 A.M. job announcing at a classical radio station, as well as juggling doctors' visits, fielding emergency calls while I was at work, while wondering if I should give up the job to stay with her full-time. After her unexpectedly sudden death, I remained with the radio work, devastated, in mourning, wondering whether my job would be my salvation or my undoing.

Each work morning was dark and tense—alarm ringing at 4 A.M., the long drive to the University of Arizona, the sound of my footsteps echoing as I walked the half mile from the parking lot to the radio station. I walked alone in the dark at 5 A.M., on guard, especially as I walked around a big TV storage truck by the KUAT entrance (I couldn't stop imagining someone lurking behind it in the darkness). By the time I'd finally unlocked the building's third door and entered the announcing booth, I'd often think, *What a setting for a murder!*

The tension didn't evaporate once inside, as a mistake in my engineering duties might interrupt the overnight "Music through the Night" feed from Minneapolis. In fact, there were countless possible engineering mistakes to make, and I'd already made most of them! My primary job was to cut off the overnight feed, open the mike, and begin introducing records, and get the Tucson day going.

Instead of opening my shift with the dull Associated Press "This Day in History" ticker, I'd gotten into the habit of doing my own version of the Gladys Taber nature columns my mother had read to me, talking to the early morning audience for a few minutes . . . sometimes about horseback rides taken, or owls heard, or sometimes I'd play the sounds of the snowy tree crickets in the bushes outside my house or birdsongs I'd recorded in the feeder in our bosque.

One early morning, listening to the overnight guy from Minneapolis end his shift, and getting ready to talk, I was stopped dead in my tracks. He was closing with the old hymn "Abide with Me," a hymn my mother often hummed in the kitchen. The hymn was so unexpected (this was a *classical* radio station, after all!) that I could hardly speak as I began on-air. I was overcome with emotion. I have no idea what I said, although I doubt if I made any reference to the hymn, but as soon as I could, I moved to the first record of the day. However, I was struck by, and somehow strangely comforted by, that lovely favorite of my mother's.

A few days later a letter from a stranger, "Grace," came to me at the station. After she told me how much the homey little bits I shared in the early morning meant to her, she asked me if I had known that "Abide with Me" was Gandhi's favorite Protestant hymn, and closed with something like, "That 'Abide with Me' morning was special to me as I felt my mother's presence very strongly." I was startled that Grace's reaction had mirrored my own.

Over the next months, in the quiet time I'd spend listening before I was on-air, I became sensitive to those moments when my mother's favorites would occasionally make surprising appearances between Beethoven and Mozart: a harp performance of her favorite, "Believe Me, If All Those Endearing Young Charms," or the Strauss waltzes that she taught me to waltz to. I told no one, but each moment of comfort, repose, and solace kept me at the job, setting the alarm for 4 A.M. each morning. And listeners became connected in a rare sense of community with my translation of my mother's Gladys Taber nature columns à la Tucson and the Southwest and would let me know, by phone calls and letters.

I began to come even earlier in the morning to await her relayed bits of music, each bringing a flow of memories and a real sense of her presence and love. However, no moment brought me closer to my mother than that first one, alone in the darkness, still overcome with sadness at her death, hearing her favorite, "Abide with Me," Gandhi's favorite hymn.

Abide with me; fast falls the eventide.
The darkness deepens; Lord with me abide.
When other helpers fail and comforts flee,
Help of the helpless, O abide with me.

A TIMELY BIRD

Joan Indelicato

Joan Indelicato is a retired reading specialist, originally from Oak Brook, Illinois. She now lives with her husband, Robert, and is a voracious reader.

My mother had congestive heart failure and I had taken a leave of absence from my teaching assignment in Illinois to be with her. She was getting progressively worse when I needed to return home to sign my teaching contract for the coming year.

The weekend I left was Father's Day, so before leaving town, I stopped and bought my dad his favorite thing—which was oysters on the half shell—and then stopped at a Marie Calendar's restaurant for my mother's beloved custard pie.

When I walked in with the oysters, my mother, who was so weak at this point that she could hardly speak, whispered, "What about me?"

"Mom, I've got a surprise for you," I said. "I just couldn't carry everything in at once."

When I returned with her custard pie, she lit up like a Christmas tree and had a twinkle in her eye, even though she was so sick.

Saturday morning, before my flight out, I told her to hang in there until I got back.

The following Monday morning I went to the high school to sign my contract. I returned home, picked up my mail, and then went up to my fifteenth-floor apartment. I had a balcony and wall-to-wall sliding glass doors that led out. Since we'd had a problem with pigeons flocking to and soiling the balcony, I was reading the mail in the living room with the drapes drawn so I couldn't see out.

Suddenly I heard this terrible racket outside, and I thought it was one of the troublesome pigeons. You can't imagine how much noise that bird was making.

I looked at the clock. It was two-fifteen in the afternoon.

Finally, when I couldn't stand it any longer, I opened the drapes and went out onto the balcony. There was a gorgeous bird outside, iridescent with blues and greens, pacing up and down on the windowsill. It was definitely not a pigeon.

Frankly, I didn't know what to make of it, so I asked the bird, "What's the problem?"

Almost immediately I became very, very sleepy. The bird continued chattering as I went inside, pulled the drapes, and went into my bedroom and fell into a very deep sleep.

There was a telephone next to my bed, and during the three to four hours I slept, I never heard it ring. I had never not heard it before.

I later learned that during this time friends had been calling and calling to tell me that my mother had died. When I finally woke up, a call came from my dad.

"Honey," he said, "where were you? We've been trying to reach you for hours." He then told me that my mother had died.

"When?" I asked.

"Twelve-fifteen."

I was so upset that I went to spend the night with my aunt and uncle. It was only in the middle of the night that I finally realized what had happened. Twelve-fifteen Tucson time was two-fifteen in Illinois. I sat straight up in bed.

"Momma, that was you," I said. "You came to say good-bye."

MAMA'S GIFTS

Lee Schnebly

Lee Schnebly, M.Ed., is a counselor specializing in individual, marriage, and family counseling. Married for forty-eight years, she is the author of three self-help books, *Nurturing Yourself and Others*, *Do It Yourself Happiness*, and *Being Happy Being Married*.

Mama died after a thirty-five year battle against lupus at age seventy-four.

Often when she and Daddy would sit out on the sunporch in the evening watching the sunset turn into night, he would say, "How about a few tunes, Bumbie?" (For years he had affectionately called her his little bumblebee, finally shortening it to simply Bumbie.)

They'd get out their harmonicas and play together, not for long, and then they'd pray a rosary and go to bed.

The sunporch was a perfect place in the evening, but come morning the heat through the glass made it unbearable. Mama periodically made curtains for the windows to use until noon or so, when the sun moved overhead.

The present curtains had hung there for some time, badly faded and needing replacement, and she would often say, "I need to go downtown and get new curtain material." But that demanded more energy than she could conjure up, and one evening her heart just stopped its hard work. She died unexpectedly but quickly.

After being married almost half a century, my dad was truly a lost soul. My brother, my husband, my daughter

Lisa, and I did the best we could to take care of the business at hand and then to restore some order to the old house at 817 Campbell where my father would continue to live.

Noticing the sorry state of the curtains, I asked if he wouldn't like for me to make new ones, since Mama had intended to do that, and he brightened.

"That would be swell," he said. "Do you think you could find some material that's blue like the Blessed Virgin wore?"

I doubted it. The marketplace in the small town they lived in had dwindled considerably after the freeway passed it by, and the only source of fabric was a tiny dime store called Rascoe's, which had a table of cheap cottons and flannels, mostly remnants of closeouts from other stores. But I hoped there might be something blue as I measured the rods that went around three walls. I would need sixteen yards of fabric that was at least forty-eight inches wide.

Driving downtown, I yearned with all my heart for any piece of fabric that long, but I seriously doubted Rascoe's would have it.

In the store, I made my way to the table and saw what I expected: plaid flannels and some calicoes and folded pieces of various one-of-a-kind yardage. And then I saw a corner of something blue. My heart racing, I pulled it out in disbelief. It was "Virgin Mary blue." Not only was it a nice heavy polyester knit, but it was 52" wide.

I measured the way Mama had taught me when I was young, pulling the fabric out to arm's length, counting how many times it would reach from my fingertips to my nose—always a good estimate of a yard.

My breathing practically stopped as I counted twelve yards, thirteen yards, fourteen, fifteen, exactly the sixteen yards I needed. I was absolutely incredulous. I hugged it close to me and breathed a prayer of thanks. Did God put it there? Or the Virgin Mary? Or was it a gift from my own mother?

I had no doubt that it was a heavenly gift, placed there to fill my father's wistful request. I raced home, eager to share with him my wonderful story, but realized as I recounted it that he wasn't grasping the unlikelihood of such a piece being available. He couldn't appreciate the rarity. But I could, and I did, and I loved sewing and hanging those curtains more than any other decorating project I ever undertook!

Poor Dad lived six more long years after that, and he was depressed the whole time. He had severe medical problems, had both legs amputated to the hips, and spent his last few years in a nursing home.

One night when he was hospitalized with pneumonia, I dreamed of Mama. I saw her dressed in a beautiful lilac dress with a cowl neck, like she sewed for herself many times, only I'd never seen her wear lilac before.

She was just beaming at me, a happy, glowing smile, with an excited radiance in her face. Then she was gone, and I awakened.

The next morning was my last visit with Daddy, and he turned his face away from me as I left. I thought it strange because he usually watched me all the way to the door.

The hospital called shortly after to tell us he'd passed away.

I wasn't surprised. I kind of knew from Mama's smile the night before that she knew she was going to get to welcome him home, and she shared her joy with me in my dream.

A few years later our daughter Laurie gave birth to our first grandchild. He was born on December 20, Mama's birthday. And his time of birth (8:17) and last name

(Campbell) matched the street address (817 Campbell) where his great-grandparents had lived.

When I heard that, I knew his great-grandmother would be watching over him his whole life, and that gift from her was the best one of all!

MIST OF LOVE

Trudy Romine

Trudy Romine, eighty-one, is a retired elementary school teacher with a background in art and music. She enjoys doing crafts for her church bazaar.

The war was eight months old when my fiancé was captured by the Japanese in the Philippines, made a POW, and died.

That same month my mother was taken into emergency surgery. She developed peritonitis, and without the benefit of sulfa drugs—the wonder drugs that were then reserved for service men and women—she subsequently died.

Soon after that I went to a small Arizona town to teach. While there I caught pneumonia. My apartment mates managed to get me into a clinic that doubled for a hospital, with two beds and a doctor's office.

I was very, very ill and I remember days of trying to come out of a haze. I looked toward the foot of my bed and saw my mother, a big, tall woman standing in a mist. "You'll be all right, honey," she said.

The mist disappeared with her and I waited for a long time for her to come back. She didn't, but her love did and I lived.

My friends thought I was crazy, but I can still see Mother whenever I need reassurance in my life.

SWEET DREAMS

Patti Williams

Patti Williams, thirty-seven, is working toward her master's degree in holistic psychology, a mind-body-spirit approach to counseling. She lives in California with her black Labrador, Reggie, and works at a community college teaching basic skills to entry-level students.

When my sisters and I lost our mother, it left a hole inside of us that was crippling. But Mom wasn't about to let it stay that way. She reached out to us the only way she knew how, and gave us the courage to move on. This is our story:

On March 24, 1986, I received a phone call from my oldest sister, who relayed that my mother, a forty-six-year-old, healthy, vivacious woman, had mysteriously slipped into a coma and was not expected to live. I boarded the next plane to Phoenix to be by her side. My two older sisters were there as well.

The first night was spent at the hospital pacing the halls and waiting impatiently for answers. It was an extraordinarily painful and confusing time because nothing made sense. Our world had been turned upside down and we were desperately seeking answers as to why.

My sisters and I took turns sitting with Mom in the ICU, listening to the machines pump air into her still body. We held her hand and talked to her, as the nurses told us that she could possibly still hear us. Her heart monitor would fluctuate whenever one of us would leave or enter the room. We sensed she knew we were there, but she just couldn't break through. It was heart wrenching.

The next day we were told by the neurologist that our mother had been deliberately poisoned with cyanide, and although all of her internal organs were functioning fine (because of the antidote she was given by the paramedics), the cyanide had reached her brain and the CAT scan was showing a straight line. They had repeated the procedure many times, and there was no question, my mother was brain dead.

The devastation we felt is indescribable. Why would anyone want to hurt our mother? She was a sweet, compassionate, wonderful woman who was loved by everyone she met. We were completely dumbfounded. As the police detective slowly filled in the details, the story began to unravel. A story of an innocent woman being in the wrong place at the wrong time.

Mom worked for a title company in Tempe, Arizona. It was a small office with only two or three other employees. One of them was a woman in a troubled marriage. Her husband was having an affair and wanted to leave, only he was broke. He devised a plan to kill his wife and collect on her life insurance so that he and his mistress could live happily ever after.

He planted cyanide in the bottled-water cooler in her office and banked on the fact that she was usually the first one to arrive in the morning. But his plan backfired. On this particular morning, my mother arrived first and drank from the water cooler before anyone else. Within a matter of seconds, she hit the floor unconscious.

The day we received the information from the doctors confirming her condition, we were all faced with a very difficult decision: Do we disconnect the life support? You may think you know what you would do if ever faced with this dilemma, but when it actually happens, it's not as cut and dried as you would expect. Letting go of your mother is one of the most painful things a woman experiences in her life, and my sisters and I were just not ready.

That night all of us stayed at my sister's house in Mesa, Arizona, where my mother had also been living. As I lay in bed the tears kept coming, and I tossed and turned all night, knowing that tomorrow we would have to make all of this a reality. I have never known such pain.

I must have dozed off, because the next thing I remember was waking myself from a horrible dream. I sat straight up and tried to catch my breath through my tears. I looked at the clock and noticed that it was exactly 2:06 A.M. I recalled that I had dreamt that I was in my mother's room at the hospital and I was standing over her bed. I leaned down to give her a kiss, and just at that moment, she popped her eyes wide open. It scared me awake.

As I sat there in the dark, I realized I was never going to get back to sleep, so I got up and headed for the kitchen. Halfway down the hall I heard voices. My sisters were up as well. Their voices were filled with much emotion as I heard both of them say, in unison, "And then her eyes popped wide open!"

Needless to say, my sisters and I felt this collective dream was a sign or message of some sort. We discussed the meaning of our dream in great detail and discovered that we had all had it at exactly the same time. When each of us awoke, we each noticed the time was precisely 2:06 A.M.

After deep contemplation, my sisters and I were all left with the same feeling in our hearts. Mom was not happy living between worlds and wanted us to let her go. The decision was made, and although it was still difficult, we were all certain that this was what she wanted and that we were doing the right thing.

As a final confirmation, when we went to see her that last day, we held her hands and told her what we had decided. As we did, her heart rate slowed to the lowest it had been since she arrived in the hospital Her face appeared peaceful, and the tense, anxious feelings we all had seemed to disappear. Mom was finally at peace. She died a short time later.

A few months later, still struggling with my loss, I had another dream. My mother came to me with a warm smile and told me all about her new life. She was happy and she wanted me to heal my heart.

The next time I spoke with my oldest sister, I shared the dream with her. She told me then that she and my other sister had also had a similar dream. From that day forward, I noticed a considerable shift in our ability to heal from this loss. After all, Mom was still here, watching and gently guiding us on our paths.

Years later, when going through old paperwork, I came across my mother's birth certificate. She was born on July 22, 1940, at 2:06 A.M. I realized then that she had decided to leave this world at the precise moment she had arrived.

I still have dreams where Mom comes to me. She doesn't always speak, but the message is always very clear: *I'm OK, I'm happy, I'm just letting you know that I am still here.* In the dreams, she is always young, always happy, and always beautiful.

One of my fondest memories of my mother is how she used to sing and hum songs all the time. She had a habit of belting out a tune when she knew the embarrassment factor would be the highest for her children. But looking back, it was truly one of the things I cherished about her.

One of her favorite songs (and now one of mine) was an old fifties tune by the Everly Brothers that went like this:

"Whenever I want you, all I have to do is dream. . . ."

THE ROCK THROWER

Donna Monthan

⌒⌒ Donna Monthan grew up in the Midwest. A former schoolteacher, she has been in real estate for the past twenty-five years. Her hobbies include reading, traveling, and investing.

My relationship with my mother before she died was not good. She was very religious. I was not. I did not believe what she believed. She was very, very evangelical.

I have two brothers and two sisters, and while I'm close to my sisters, only the youngest one shared my mother's beliefs.

About three years ago my sisters and I decided that it was necessary to put Mother in a nursing home, so the three of us went to Kansas, where she lived. My brothers opted not to go, since they didn't want to have anything to do with the process.

Before I left my home in Tucson, I decided that I didn't want to wear my Rolex watch, so I bought a twenty-dollar watch to wear on the trip. I joined my sisters in Kansas and we did what had to be done and then returned a couple of months later and sold all of Mother's things that wouldn't go with her to the nursing home.

I found that I liked the cheap little watch with the black leather strap, and I was wearing it a lot, especially when I wore black.

A year and a half later Mother's health got worse. Finally the time came when my two sisters and I knew that she wasn't going to last more than two to three days. Although I was unable to get an airline reservation, my youngest sister was in Kansas with my mother and kept us apprised of her declining condition.

That morning I left my house, knowing that my mother did not have long to live. I knew that bad news would come within twenty-four hours. I was driving and crying when I looked down and saw that my little black watch had quit running.

I stopped at a store for a new battery and then found myself saying, "I think my mother died this morning." This was on March 30.

When I stopped for gas, it started hailing on me—unusual for Tucson at the end of March. I met my husband for lunch and told him that I'd been crying all morning, and then I said, "I feel so peaceful. I know Mother has died."

My sister called a couple of hours later and said that Mother had died at the same exact time—given the time changes—that my watch had stopped. She said that when she left the hospital in Kansas, it had been hailing. It turned out that that was the same time that it hailed on me, many states away.

I always told my mother, I don't believe what you believe. You'll have to show me a sign."

She did. She threw rocks at us!

On the first anniversary of my mother's death, my adult daughter was in the hospital in Phoenix. I was quite concerned about her. Earlier in the month I had torn a ligament in my ankle and was wearing an air brace.

I went into the grocery store to buy some fresh flowers. Another woman was also looking over the bouquets, and we started discussing which ones we liked the best. Suddenly she turned to me and said, "Your angel wants me to tell you not to worry, everything will be all right."

Thinking she had noticed my ankle brace, I said, "Oh, it's nothing but a torn ligament."

"Not that," she said. "You are worried about something else and it will turn out fine. You can be concerned, but don't worry."

I told the stranger I *was* worried about my daughter. I hugged her and then left the store not knowing her name. I've never seen her again.

I felt strongly that my mother was trying to comfort me that day. In the past, I had frequently confided in her and she had always given me good advice. Now, after her death, in some extraordinary way she was able to send a woman I had never seen before to reassure me.

And of course, she was right. My daughter turned out to be fine.

IF YOU SEE A HEART

Roxanne Hawbaker

Roxanne Hawbaker, forty-nine, is a legal secretary. In her spare time she enjoys singing, oil painting, and working with her church.

At my mother's knee as a little child, I would gaze into her face as she played the piano and sang loving melodies: "A little turned-up nose, two cheeks just like a rose, so sweet from head to toe, that little girl of mine . . . two eyes that shine so bright, two lips that kiss good night, two arms that hold me tight, that little girl of mine." As her soothing voice caressed my very soul, the notes dropped gently into my heart and forever bonded securely the strong love between us. Even now, my heart thrills at the remembrance of this love so freely given and so deeply felt.

A dedicated preacher's wife, Mother followed my father to pioneer a church far away from her own dear family and the Colorado Rockies she loved so much. There were struggles over the years, which my brothers and I felt but could not fully comprehend. Yet, as she taught us to look to God for answers, she would say, "Look for the clouds with the silver linings," and she would play and sing, "God is the answer to all our problems, God is the answer to all our needs . . ." to uplift her soul, thus lifting and directing ours ever heavenward.

Her morning devotionals were always, "Let no one hurt us, and let us hurt no one." In the evening it was, "We pray for those we should pray for but may not know about." She really covered all the bases with those two daily prayers!

Years later, when our father divorced our mother, much joy left Mother's blue eyes, and I could hear heavy sadness in her voice. It was our family love, that binding together, that had made us understand God's perfect love, so simple yet true. Now she, who had gladdened our hearts so many times, was filled with pain. How could I now lift her up?

I prayed for a special way to express the depth of my love for her. One day I found two red alabaster hearts, each about the size of my hand. Giving one to Mother, I told her whenever she looked at it, she would know I'd be thinking of her and to remember how much I loved her. Likewise, whenever I looked at mine, I would know Mother would be thinking of me and loving me even more.

Thereafter, on holidays, special occasions, and some-times "just because," we started giving each other some-thing heart-shaped or with hearts on it, be it a T-shirt with hearts on it or a coffee cup with a heart-shaped handle. It became an unspoken theme between us: "If you see a heart, you'll know I'm thinking of you, you'll know I love you." We started taking turns "hearting" each other.

The heart theme started touching others too. When we moved into our new home in September last year, my hus-band surprised me one morning, as he took my hand and led me into our yet unlandscaped backyard, where he had grown an eight-foot-wide grass heart—he was so proud of our home! It was a sincere expression of love. Mother had helped us move—she got such a big smile on her face when we showed her that grass heart together!

Just this last Christmas, among the other presents, I gave Mother a straw heart-shaped potholder. Chandra, my then seven-year-old daughter, helped me find it for her Grandma Vel. Their grandmother-granddaughter love also became bound deeper in the "heart game" we played. Wanting to share the "heart love" with my daughter, we had sewn many colored hearts onto a denim jacket for Chandra. In January of this year, she lost that jacket at school. We checked everywhere, especially the lost-and-found table in the hall, nearly every day. No one turned it in and we prayed for its return.

On March 5, Grandma Vel agreed to pick Chandra up because an emergency faculty meeting would keep her father late and I would still be working. Mother knew about the missing heart jacket. She told me later that on her way to get Chandra, she said a prayer that whoever had it would return it. As Mother passed the lost-and-found table, there was the jacket! Now, don't you find it wonderfully unique that God answered our prayers for the return of that jacket in His own particular time after Mother's prayer, so that when Chandra came out of her schoolroom door, there was Grandma Vel holding out her special heart jacket, giving her love and a heart memory to treasure?

The heart game had started a couple of years before God had blessed us, after waiting twelve long years, with our little daughter, Chandra. Finally having my own daughter deepened my understanding of this mother-daughter love. Not a greater love than others, certainly not greater than God's love for us—He, after all, made love possible. But, as I explained to my daughter, when she asked, in a four-year-old's innocence, who I loved most, God or her, "Well," I said, "God first, but not exactly the most; it's a different, separate love." She accepted that and understood it.

Love of husband, father-daughter love, etc., it's all wonderful, but mother-daughter love is so special. I was amazed anew that my own mother could love me as much as I love my own daughter, as I was so new at experiencing its depths.

During this last Christmas season, one Sunday during worship, God gave me a vision of heaven. Although I had had a vision years ago, after my grandmother had gone to heaven, of many celestial figures ascending and descending glorious stairways, this vision was of the most busy, energetic, yet positive and bright place. It was so real that the scene shocked me, panicked me that maybe I was going to go there. I just didn't want that right now, not when I was experiencing such closeness to my daughter, my mother, my husband, and others.

Then, while I was singing in our praise services in church, I began consistently hearing my maternal grandmother, who had died in 1990, singing beside me. Hearing her voice with such clarity, I had to stop singing and turn my head to see if she was there.

I remember now that my mother had mentioned that she had heard Grandmother singing too, several times. Mother missed her beloved parents so much. I understood that she loved her mother as much as I loved her. These mother-daughter love bonds were just seemingly handed down and spilled over.

Although my grandmother went to Heaven at the age of ninety-two, my maternal grandfather died at the age of only fifty-nine, of a heart attack in 1960, the year after my baby brother was born. Mother had been deeply affected by his death back then. Although I was only nine, I remember saying good-bye to his earthly body, yet knowing fully in my soul that he was alive in heaven.

Mother had instilled those living love truths in us, and all my trials and errors and answers to youthful prayers had convinced me that we do, indeed, live, after death, in Christ. It was an undeniable knowledge in my soul, even at that young age, that death was only temporary.

Yet these many years later, my mother-daughter love yearned to impart and instill that truth to my own daughter. And I still wanted to express the depth of love I held in my heart for my own beloved mother.

Mother shared *The Christmas Box* by Richard Evans with us. This was a simple story illuminating again the realization that through God's great love for each of us human beings, He made a way so there would be no more death or sorrow, and we could, one glorious day, have a reunion together and we would not have to be parted.

With the busy times everyone gets tied up in, I prayed for windows of time to spend with my mother. I was working full-time, rushing home to be with my husband and daughter, trying to do my part with Sunday school and church activities, and it seemed Mother always waited patiently for my time, and yet she readily joined in to help us share holidays and special times. We were closer than ever in our love.

On Good Friday my dear mother had a massive heart attack. The realization that I could be losing Mother, that God had been preparing my heart for the separation, that Grandmother was preparing for Mother's grand homecoming, finally set in. I did not hear Grandmother singing any more after that.

The doctor felt Mother's diabetes had weakened her heart to the extent that they could not do surgery. Yet, after eight days in the hospital, we got to take her home. I spent a wonderful two days with her and she seemed to be doing better, but I had to go to work that Monday morning, April 7. I had spoken to her on the telephone before my brothers arrived (a miracle in itself that, with their flying schedules, they could both be there with her at the same time).

They phoned me before I went to lunch at noon that Mother seemed in distress; they could not get a pulse or even blood pressure and were probably going to take her back to the hospital, yet she was still talking.

I was waiting for my boss to return to the office so I could tell him I had to leave. Alone, as I tried to eat my lunch, I began praying that, if God would not heal Mother completely, He would at least not let her suffer. I had my left hand on the table so I could watch the time. Suddenly I felt someone touch that hand. At the same time, I felt Mother's sweet presence, so real, and an indescribable peace. I knew in my heart of hearts that she was taking her walk with the Lord to heaven. I noted the time as 12:40 P.M.

At 1 P.M. my younger brother called and told me to get to the hospital as soon as possible. When I arrived, my older brother met me at the emergency room and told me they had not been able to revive her. As I kissed her sweet face and hands, I asked the nurse what time they had logged her losing consciousness. They had 12:41!

So you see, my beloved mother told me good-bye, as she would so often not go anywhere without first telling me where she'd be. And the good Lord had not let her suffer. She had had some discomfort in her chest, but He had let her systems shut gently down, one by one, as He called her home.

After my beloved mother went to heaven (I will not say "died," you understand, knowing she is more alive there than ever before) and several days after the funeral, my brothers and I read and sorted through the many boxes of magazine clippings, letters, etc., that Mother had saved all those years. Missing her was just too much. Now, as I sorted through all these things she had lovingly saved for her children, family, friends—things she had wanted to share—I recounted her touch on my hand in farewell. How could I let her go? Because we were so close, the void was just too painful.

Suddenly I lifted up a few papers clipped together with a small gold metal heart-shaped bookmark. It was as if she reached out just then with it to say, "There, I'm here, I still love you!" When had she put that there? My brothers could have come across it instead of me, of course, but they didn't. I found it. It was planned just for me and it is like a small piece of jewelry that I wear as a pin in fond remembrance.

The Lord plans such wonderful surprises for His children—only He can put such detail together in such a masterful plan for the right place and the right time. Only He could take this special gift between my beloved mother and me and plan such a wonderful story to share, to remind me and you, now reading this, that the love is still there and will always be.

Mother waits for me up there, yet I still come across hearts now and then to remind me that she still loves me. For instance, a few days later, again feeling alone without her, as I dutifully sorted and gently touched her things, I reached up to see if a closet shelf was empty, and my hand touched a small object. I discovered it was a piece of cedar wood made into a heart! I was so elated, it was as if she had just kissed me!

Another week went by and as I went tearfully through some boxes of her more personal and precious things, although I had looked at each handkerchief of hers we kept, my eye spotted one I had not seen before—white with little red hearts all over it. Oh, how I clasped that to my heart, drinking in the sudden love from her that overwhelmed me just then. You see, she has not let me do this loving duty of sorting alone. It's as if she's still by my side and "hearts" me to help me through it.

Just last week, as my little daughter and I lovingly went through her clothes, we checked pockets. Chandra knew Grandma often put special little treats in pockets. As I pulled a red scarf out of a front pocket of a pantsuit, I nearly cried with joy as a silver heart-shaped button fell out into my hand. I noticed then that the garment had other heart-shaped buttons that Mother had sewn on. We had found them together just last year. What a wonderful memory of shopping together with Mother that was! And there she was again, telling me she's thinking of me and loving me still.

It's an ongoing thing, you see. Her heart up there is still as full of love for us as before, and we are drawn ever closer in the promise of our eternal reunion with Mother and others we love so dearly.

So if you see a heart, think of your loved ones' hearts, so full of love for you still, waiting to show us on that glorious day all the wonders they already know in heaven, where love begins and never ends. It's that comfort and love that fills our hearts afresh.

And if you think this story has an ending, remember, love never ends. Just this morning as I put on a garment that I had saved that was Mother's (thinking I would be closer to her if I wore something of hers), I turned around in the mirror and there, on one side, was sewn a flowered heart! I had not seen that when I went through her things. So she has "hearted" me again.

Thank you, Mother, for your continuing reminders of your love, your little heart gifts. They thrill my heart with your constant love. And thank you, God, for my wonderful mother!

LIFE OF SPIRIT

Cheryl Booth

〜 Cheryl Booth is a psychic medium and hypnotherapist. Fifteen years ago she sat in the same psychic development circle as James Van Praagh. In fact, they were both mentored by the British medium Brian Hurst. Her book, *Brother John, My Guardian Angel,* is about her astounding communication with her brother after his death. A gifted teacher, Cheryl offers classes in mediumship and psychic development. Her hypnotherapy practice includes past life regression, hypno-channeling, releasing phobias, and positive behavior modifications.

When my brother was born, he suffered from what they called in those days "birth defects." Actually what he had was severe cerebral palsy. He never walked nor did he speak probably more than five words, yet he was the most evolved angel in a human guise that I ever knew.

My mother's name was Dolores, which means pain in Spanish. In many ways she fulfilled the sad promise of her name in her physical life. Mother blamed herself for Johnny's physical problems. Feeling that his birth defects were her fault because she was forty-three when she had him, she took on the guilt for his condition.

We were brought up in the Pentecostal Church, and the ministers there laid hands on my brother sometimes three times a week. The purpose was, of course, to have him get up and walk, but he never did.

I was a very psychic child and my precognitive dreams

frightened my mother. When I was twelve, she told me to stop what I was doing psychically.

It was also during this time that I realized that Johnny was very happy exactly the way he was. I tried to explain this to my mother, but she would never accept it.

Mother died young, of cancer at the age of fifty-four, when I was fifteen. My brother, Johnny, was eleven, and when she left it was at a time when we really needed her.

After her death my mother came through in a reading for me done by James Van Praagh. She told me that in the spirit world there are different dimensions, or neighborhoods, and that she and my father were in the same one.

Through my years of spiritual work it is my understanding that there are as many different levels of spiritual awareness in the spirit world as there are here on earth. Like attracts like, so spirits with the same awareness and levels of understanding hang out together.

"Your father and I are stunned," my mother said. "We're so amazed at your brother, John. He is such an evolved soul. Although he comes for visits, he's in another area where he is studying with master teachers like Christ and Buddha."

She went on to tell me how honored they were to have had John in their lives. "With our limited understanding on earth," she said, "we thought that we were given custody of this poor little crippled child. Now we know that he was there to teach us."

So her biggest gift to me was her understanding that John was a highly evolved spirit and that our perceptions here on earth are not always what they seem.

Over the years, I've found that contacting loved ones in the spirit world can be very healing. For one thing, contact helps people release the attachment to whatever was left unsaid. If things were not pleasant the last time two people interacted here, once people are in spirit they no longer hold a grudge, realizing that to do so is a waste of energy.

I've also learned that spirits can manifest whatever environments they want out of etherea.

To contact your loved ones in the spirit world, you don't really need a medium. You can communicate with them through thoughts, the spoken word, and through writing letters to them. They hear you and they will respond to your thoughts, especially when you're doing activities that they like to do.

Another effective way to start the communication is right before you go to sleep at night, to ask them to come to you in a dream. That way you'll meet on neutral ground.

Remember, your loved ones are drawn to you, and through your mutual love you can keep talking to them. And please bear in mind that visiting a medium is not a substitute for grief counseling. If that would be beneficial, I recommend that you seek a professional group or counselor to assist you in moving forward with your own life.

Celebrate the times you spent with those who have passed. My understanding is that they have moved beyond their pain and that they encourage you to do the same.

Be thankful and aware of the blessings that surround you each and every day. That includes gratitude for the love and time shared with those now in spirit, and realizing that we are never truly separated from them.

A GLIMPSE AT A WONDERFUL PLACE

Martha Lawrence

Martha Lawrence, forty-four, is the author of the popular mystery series featuring psychic detective Elizabeth Chase. Inspired by her own real-life psychic experiences, *Murder in Scorpio* won her nominations for the Edgar, Agatha, and Anthony awards in 1996. It was followed by the critically acclaimed sequels *The Cold Heart of Capricorn*, *Aquarius Descending*, *Pisces Rising*, and *The Ashes of Aries*. Martha's novels have been published around the world.

I probably come from a long line of highly intuitive women. My mother was certainly psychic. She once balked at an airport gate and refused to let our family get on a flight to Jamaica because she "knew" the plane would crash. It did, killing everyone on board.

She passed that ability on to me. The mystery series I write—featuring a psychic detective—is based on my own paranormal experiences.

In December 1999 my mother and I knew that she was dying of terminal cancer. Since we were both psychic, I wanted to approach the subject of her contacting me after she crossed over. With this thought in mind, I sat at her side and began:

"Mom, I've been thinking..."

But she read my mind before I could finish the sentence.

"I'll try," she said. "I can't promise I'll be able to contact you after I go, but I promise you I'll try." Her telepathy startled and delighted me; I had to laugh.

Mom went into a coma a few days after that conversation. I sat at her side, holding her hand. It felt as if she'd already left her body—she barely had a pulse and her skin was cold. She'd been comatose for about five hours when suddenly I felt her come back into her body. She sat up, opened her eyes, and gave me the brightest, most joyful smile I'd ever seen on her face.

"It's wonderful!" she said, telling me about where she'd been. "It's . . . wonderful." I could see the awe and amazement in her eyes as she struggled to find words for the experience. "There's . . . my mother . . . and bees . . ." Her joy was palpable, infectious. My mother was dying, yet at that moment I felt elated, touched by a power much greater than myself. I put my arms around her and snuggled closer.

"I love you, Mom," was all I could think to say.

With what little strength she could muster, she patted my shoulder.

"Aw," she said, "my baby."

She closed her eyes and slipped away for good that time. But she left me the best possible gift—the knowledge that her destination was indeed a glorious one.

Afterword ∾

> *Now faith is being sure of what we hope*
> *for and certain of what we do not see.*
>
> —HEBREWS 11:1

Children, perhaps because they have not yet been stifled by convention or science, are frequently receptive to afterlife signs.

I was speaking in Homer, Alaska, not long ago and reading the "June First" story from this book. In the audience was a well-behaved baby who was awake, but very quiet. When I got to the part about my mother's actually taking her last breath, the baby suddenly sat up and said, "Bye-bye, Momma, bye-bye."

I've often wondered how many of our children's "invisible" playmates and imaginary friends are really people who have gone to the spirit world and are checking back in with the younger members of their families.

My cousin Lauri has a daughter, Lindsey, who had one such imaginary playmate, a friend she called John. My cousin would hear her young daughter talking to John, and oftentimes Lindsey would share details of John's life with her mother.

When Lindsey was fourteen, she and her mother were looking through some old family pictures and came across a photo of a young couple in their twenties. They were wearing white and the man was very handsome and tan. It was our grandmother's brother, John Pegg, who died in 1955, years before Lindsey was born.

She picked up the picture and studied it. "That's John," she said. "He's dead? My friend John is dead?"

She couldn't believe it. For there, in the old black-and-white photograph, was indeed her friend John, the same John whom she had spent hours talking to and playing with.

She hadn't known he was dead. She just knew that he was her friend.

I mentioned earlier that although the focus of this book was afterlife gifts from mothers to daughters, the communication is possible between anyone who is in the spirit world and anyone here on earth.

But it goes beyond the human realm.

Last week I had to put my beloved cockapoo to sleep. Adopted from the Humane Society when she was a year old, Missy had been with me for thirteen years. Every day when I went to my office to write, Missy was there beside me, sleeping on the Navajo rug. Ever cheerful, she was our social director, insisting that all of the animals and people in her kingdom get along. She was also an inspiration to me in that she was the model for the dog Mrs. Fierce who appears in my mystery books.

While just as I know that my mother is all right in the spirit world, I also know that Missy is having a grand time chasing rabbits, getting into the trash, or hiding Milk-Bones from God. Still, I miss her.

The afternoon of her death, through my heart-shattering

grief, I asked (out loud, *always* out loud) for her to give me a sign that she was well. A short time later I found her striped rawhide candy cane behind the couch cushions. Late that afternoon I rescued two hunting dogs from a busy highway and returned them to their owner, and then my aunt, who had not been told of Missy's passing, mentioned that she thought she would adopt a dog from the Humane Society.

The next morning, greedy for yet more communication from Missy, I said, "I know you're all right, but are you having fun?" That afternoon I found Mao the cat's stuffed veterinarian (which she delights in thumping with her back feet) in the middle of my desk. It had never left our bedroom before.

All coincidence? I don't think so. It was Missy's way of letting me know she was all right and that she was, indeed, having fun.

M. Scott Peck writes in *The Road Less Traveled and Beyond:*

> It is a major thesis of mine that grace, manifested in part by "valuable or agreeable things not sought for," is available to everyone. But while some take advantage of it, others do not.
>
> One of the reasons for the human tendency to resist grace is that we are not fully aware of its presence. We don't find valuable things not sought for because we fail to appreciate the value of the gift when it is given to us.

And sometimes we fail to recognize the gifts that are sent to us. Lots of messages are being sent and are being returned to sender because we simply don't pay attention. We don't trust that first intuitive burst of knowingness. Instead, we brush it off or chalk it up to our imaginations and in so doing we cheat ourselves out of some of the best gifts we will ever have.

Obviously there are some pretty strict rules up there, or over there, or wherever that other side is located. Apparently spirits are not allowed to write in dust on cars, or leave letters in mailboxes, or draw diagrams on boards. Since the rules are somewhat skewed, those of us left behind must also put what we think to be true in abeyance and let the impressions just come in.

Trust and believe in the thoughts that come to you. Have faith in the first impressions that come in. This is not the time to be analytical or critical of the process. That can come later. If you cultivate an open mind, you will be surprised and pleased at what will come through.

While we may not be able to summon these communications at will, it certainly doesn't hurt to ask.

Conversely, there will be times when we have not asked for a communication, nor have we been thinking about a loved one who has died, and we will still receive some kind of afterlife gift.

I often receive unexpected communications from the spirit world. I suppose, since I haven't been thinking of the person involved, these gifts should be anonymous, but they're not. There is a sudden flash of their memory that tells me where the communication is coming from. Somehow I disengage my left brain, in fact maybe my entire brain, and let the feelings come in without censure.

While I can't say with any certainty how or even if a particular message will be sent, the following suggestions may help the process.

First, ask. Ask the person in the spirit world to contact you. While your request doesn't have to be complicated, it does have to be made *out loud*. Spirits want to contact us, but they get discouraged when we don't speak to them or when we don't hear their messages. By asking out loud, we are not only being "heard" in the spirit world, but we are acknowledging that we are eager to receive any messages that they may want to send.

If you don't get a message, don't be shy about asking again. Sometimes even spirits need to speak up.

I have a good friend who was very skeptical of this book and the processes described in it. But her skepticism could not overcome the disappointment she felt that her own mother had never checked in with her. After asking—out loud—for a contact, her mother did just that. Her heartwarming story is told in "A Skeptic Checks In."

Now I find myself asking a lot. Usually it's for insignificant things, like asking, "Mother, I'm speaking on *Feathers* tonight and I'd really like to wear that black top; can you help me find it?" Or I'll ask my grandmother who loved fine textiles, "Could you help me find the Christmas table runner?" Again, I don't know the how and why of it, but I do know that it works and the blouse or the table runner always turns up.

Meditation or even doing any number of things that put us on automatic pilot, such as running, driving a car, or swimming, can help us receive afterlife gifts. The more we use our subconscious to know ourselves, the more we will be in tune with the cosmos.

Remember that no one can enlighten you but yourself.

Sometimes seeds of truth are planted, but will not sprout until the conditions are right. While I can tell you what I believe to be true, you will not believe until the time is right for you, if ever. For my truth may not necessarily be your truth.

But what each of us has, deep within ourselves, is a truth barometer, an internal mechanism that either strikes a chord or doesn't.

I have learned over the years that a simple, but important component of my truth barometer is goose bumps.

Yep. Simple run-up-your-arms, chills-down-your-spine goose bumps.

I've discovered that they are an affirmation and that what I am thinking, reading, or experiencing is true.

I suspect that you will also learn to trust your goose bumps.

As you begin to trust, you will discover that the intuition welled deep within your body is the wisest wisdom of all.

This book began with a chapter titled "Genesis," which signifies the birth of something. What I have tried to propose here, with the help of all the women who have contributed their wonderful stories, is that death is never an ending, but rather a beginning of a new and beautiful communication from spirit. All that is really required is that we listen with open hearts and minds and accept the grace that is offered to us.

May peace and love be with you.

SINCLAIR BROWNING

The Spirit World ～

Henry Jackson Van Dyke, an American preacher, poet, and philosopher in the early 1900s, wrote one of my favorite pieces on life after death.

A Parable of Immortality

I am standing upon the seashore. A ship by my side spreads her white sails to the morning breeze and starts for the blue ocean. She is an object of beauty and strength and I stand and watch until at last she hangs like a speck of a white cloud just where the sea and sky come down to mingle with each other. Then someone by my side says, "There she goes!"

Gone where? Gone from my sight . . . that is all. She is just as large in mast and hull and spar as she was when she left my side and just as able to bear her load of living freight to the place of destination. Her diminished size is in me, not in her.

And just at the moment where someone at my side says, "There she goes!" there are other eyes watching her and other voices ready to take up the glad shout, "There she comes!"

Wouldn't it be great if those who have left us could leave letters in our mailboxes, or detailed messages on our answering machines? Definite, irrefutable signs that would tell us what they were encountering on the other side? If only . . . Ah, the mystery of life . . . and death.

For now, we must be content with what our mothers choose to tell us about their lives after life.

The Power of Sharing ～

In editing this book I have learned many lessons. One of the most important of them is that when even one person is willing to come forward and say, "This is what happened to me and I am not afraid to tell you this story," great things can and will happen.

As I have spoken around the country, sharing the stories I have been entrusted with, I have been met with nodding heads, smiles, and tears as listeners have begun sharing their secret stories.

If you have an afterlife gift story (from your brother, sister, mother, father, child, pet, etc.) that you would like to be considered for a future book, feel free to contact me. Please include your story, your name, address, telephone number, and e-mail address if you have one.

Sinclair Browning
P.O. Box 8248
Tucson, AZ 85738

Suggested Reading ～

Browne, Sylvia, with Lindsey Harrison. *Life on the Other Side: A Psychic's Tour of the Afterlife.* New York: Dutton, 2000.

Browne, Sylvia, with Lindsey Harrison. *The Other Side and Back: A Psychic's Guide to Our World and Beyond.* New York: Dutton, 1999.

Day, Laura. *Practical Intuition.* New York: Villard Books, Random House, 1996.

Garfield, Patricia, Ph.D. *The Dream Messenger.* New York: Simon & Schuster, 1997.

Guggenheim, Bill, and Judy Guggenheim. *Hello From Heaven!* New York: Bantam Books, 1996.

Hampton, Charles. *The Transition Called Death: A Recurring Experience.* Wheaton, Illinois: Quest Books, 1994.

Kübler-Ross, Elisabeth. *On Death and Dying.* New York: Simon and Schuster, 1997.

Linn, Denise. *The Secret Language of Signs.* New York: Ballantine Books, 1996.

Martin, Joel, and Patricia Romanowski. *We Don't Die*. New York: G.P. Putnam's Sons, 1988.

Moody, Raymond, M.D. *Reunions: Visionary Encounters with Departed Loved Ones*. New York: Villard Books, 1993.

Moody, Raymond A., Jr. *Life After Life*. New York: Bantam Books, 1988.

Smith, Susy. *Life Is Forever*. New York: Dell Publishing Co., 1977.

Van Praagh, James. *Talking to Heaven*. New York: Dutton, 1997.

Wilson, Ian. *The After Death Experience*. New York: William Morrow and Co., 1987.

About the Editor ~~

Sinclair Browning is the author of the Trade Ellis mystery series, several historical novels, and is the coauthor of a horse-training book. One of five nominees for the 2000 Arizona Arts Award, Browning lives in the country outside of Tucson, Arizona, with her husband and assorted menagerie.

You can find out more about Sinclair Browning through her Web site:

sinclairbrowning.com